I hope you enjoy this
as much as I did writing
it!

Best Wishes

Andy

INNKEEPING WITH
MR. FAWLTY

A Four Leaf Clover Book

Cover illustration by Nigel Paige.

A catalogue record for this book is available from the British Library.

ISBN: 0 954 88836 7   Hardback

0 954 88837 5   Soft Cover

An imprint of La Fontaine Media
49560 France.

www.lafontainepress.com

The Menu

To Jemma and Emily with love from your Pop. Please read this when you are a little older, my special ones.

Introduction

When I was aged just ten, Fawlty Towers entertained my father and older brothers, but its fictional humour frustrated my mother. I was too young to understand many of the nuances and innuendos, so I just laughed at the mad-looking stick insect of a man doing silly things to even harder-to-believe guests and staff. I found some of the stories unbelievable – that is, until I took over the reins of Mortons House Hotel, a sixteenth-century manor house in Corfe Castle, Dorset in southern England.

Basil Fawlty may not be a figure you would think it sensible to aspire to, nor to be compared with; however, having accommodated a few Germans, hotel inspectors, unmarried lovers, doctors and wrongly identified spoon salesmen myself, comparisons start there. I have a great deal of sympathy with the much-maligned Mr. Fawlty, because very few people can ever understand the stresses and strains the industry puts upon the hotelier and, like him, I now need a psychiatrist.

However careful you are to plan ahead, things can and do go pear shaped, as guests *can be that bad* and staff can seriously screw up and let you down just at the wrong moment. All the time, like Basil, I am expected to smile obsequiously throughout the process. Acting 24/7 is tough and sometimes impossible to carry off with any success, as eventually the stress gets too much and you inevitably 'blow your stack.'

In many ways it takes a personality just like the proprietor of the fictional hotel in Torquay to run a hotel – and Sybil is, of course, an essential cog in the works.

Andy Hageman

Mortons House circa 1900

1

Celebrity Boots

"**W**here can I dry these?" she said in the sort of Roedean accent affected by television presenters when in the presence of their inferiors.

I gazed at 'these' and 'these' gazed back at me, soggily.

They were a pair of hiking boots, jolly hockey stick sort of footwear, just the thing for tramping through the gorse and heather and the hillsides of the English countryside and coastline. Unfortunately, they seemed to have missed out on the gorse and heather. What they had collected, in large quantities, was some of our best Dorsetshire mud and Jurassic sand, suitably mixed with an ample percentage of the rain that had been falling steadily for the past few days. Actually, much of it had not been falling, since a howling gale had contrived to move a good deal of it horizontally.

The mixture oozed from the lace holes and uppers, descending onto my reception desk where it was forming artistic pools of what is known in the painting trade as yellow ochre or perhaps burnt umber.

Now, her 'boot stand' was hand crafted in solid Oak and had only recently been installed as our front desk for some 11,000 quid, a fair price for a bit of polished woodwork. The craftsman who had fixed it had eulogised on the sort of hard wear it would take over the years but, to my knowledge, he had never mentioned it as being a suitable place to dry a pair of muddy hiking boots, even with an odour *célébrité* attached to them.

The owner of the aforementioned boots was what passes these days for a celebrity of the television screen and radio star. She and a film crew had descended on us while they were making a film of a walk along the Jurassic coast. Although we only take two night bookings at weekends, they assured us that we would get an honourable mention in The Daily 'Another Newspaper' for our hospitality if we just put them up for one night.

It is a fact of life that hoteliers are held responsible for the weather and this weekend was no exception. We failed. Guests faced with torrential downpours become moody, sullen and argumentative and no amount of Scrabble in front of a log fire can lift their spirits. TV personalities, forced to get on with filming in what appeared to be the monsoon season, having struggled in the teeth of a gale for the better part of the day, see no reason not to blame their host. And as the weather and hence the state of her boots were clearly my fault, it was, in her eyes, my duty to take care of the matter. There was a raindrop forming on the end of her nose and she was of a healthy pink hue from having been out in the wind for a few hours.

"Not there, love," I said firmly, with a look of disdain. And *most* reluctantly, given her resultant glare, I removed them to a more suitable place to dehydrate, namely the boiler room.

I suppose TV personalities are used to having their every whim taken care of without question. Minions exit their presence backwards, bowing obsequiously, and my comment clearly came as a bit of a shock to her system. She certainly seemed taken aback and I felt sure that my television licence would be revoked forthwith as she stormed off, looking for a less irascible staff member, if not for boot drying, then licking.

Some fool once opined, 'The customer is always right.' Obviously, he had not been in the leisure hotel business.

But the rest of the evening went with a bit of a swing. There was an even bigger and better known television personality present who became the life and soul of the party over dinner. Like the captain of a cruise ship, I joined them at their table and contributed a few merry quips, only to be deflated on catching the eye of my lady of the boots. She seemed to be eyeing me with the sort of gaze that old hunters on safari had on spying a likely bit of game on the horizon, a narrowing of the eyes. And on hearing my voice, her expression changed to that of someone chewing on a wasp.

My aunt had flown in from America for a short stay and had an interesting conversation with the major television personality present without revealing her relationship to the owner. He seemed extremely pleased with the hotel and the standard of service and, along with the rest of the crew, expressed his thanks before leaving. There was, however, one exception. My lady of the boots refused to have even eye contact with me despite her now having a toasty warm and dry pair, courtesy of me.

Some time later, we heard that *that* newspaper was running the article on the event in which we would be featured.

I ordered ten copies from our local newsagent in anticipation, proudly mentioning that we would be featured.

We were.

Unfortunately, my booted friend had penned the article. It read:

"Mortons House Hotel is a fine old building in the centre of Corfe Castle and was supervised on the night we stayed there by a man who clearly thought Fawlty Towers was a management training video."

She went on to say nice things about the food, the beds and the staff, but ended by saying: "It's just that Basil is not nearly as funny in real life."

This did, of course, give rise to a good deal of mirth locally and amongst the staff, but as there's no such thing as bad publicity it was no surprise that many new guests came to visit subsequently just for the experience and to test Basil.

It wasn't the first time that I had been compared to Mr Fawlty, as is my wife to Sybil.

And it was certainly not to be the last.

When I left school for the last time in 1982, the then-deputy head said that I would never amount to anything and be of no use to society whatsoever! But now I am being compared to the great Basil Fawlty. Diary note to self – Practice Goose-step.

Basil Fawlty. It's something to live up to – and I've done my best ever since!

2.

An Inspector Calls

I was gazing thoughtfully at the ruined Castle from the desk within my newly acquired Elizabethan manor, pondering on all the squire duties I had ahead of me, when the phone rang.

"There's a lady to see you," the receptionist downstairs said in a sort of stage whisper.

"A lady?"

"Says she's from the Environmental Health Department."

"Oh, Lord, I'd forgotten they might show up. A lady you said?"

We had only been in residence at Mortons House for a few weeks and, although I knew we were overdue for an inspection, in the heat of battle I had forgotten all about it.

I had rather envisioned the inspector as being a tweedy, pipe-smoking old buffer, and my plan was to wheel him into the bar for a couple of stiff gins. After a man-to-man chat about food, health, safety and, I suppose, a bit about all the paperwork we should be completing, he would clap me on the back and tell me what a fine establishment we had, before shuffling off back to Purbeck District Council. I might even offer him lunch.

But now, with a female to deal with, clearly Plan A had gone out the window.

Colin, my General Manager, or Beverley, my Reception Manager could have handled the situation perfectly but today was their day off and I was the only one to face the slings and arrows of outrageous bureaucracy. They alone would have known how to deal with this female inspector and would have had all the answers, having worked at Mortons House for some considerable time. For myself, I doubted that I would even understand the questions, as, at my first establishment, others dealt with such things.

For Plan B I summoned up all my not-inconsiderable skills honed during my earlier profession as a purveyor of extremely expensive cars to extremely expensive people. Beaming effusively, I sashayed into reception.

"What a beautiful day you picked to come and visit us," I warbled. She looked ominously like one of my old school teachers. She glared back at me, as if I had delayed too long with another homework assignment.

"You are the manager here?"

"No, no, Madam. I am the owner and new squire of the manor," I said lightly. "My manager and manageress both have the day off, so I will do my best to cover for them."

She sniffed as though she suspected something was wrong with the drains, my head, or like someone who had already found a caterpillar in the Lollo Rosso.

"First, I need somewhere to change."

"To change?"

"Of course. You would hardly expect me to do an inspection dressed like this."

I ushered her into the ladies cloakroom and made a mad dash through the kitchen, by now empty of chefs who were on their break. All looked in good order, the carnage of breakfast had been cleared and all was well, I felt. It looked clean enough anyway.

I was nervous and with good reason. Mortons House was not my first venture into what is laughingly referred to as the hospitality business. That had been in a small hotel or upmarket B&B, called Dial House, in partnership with my brother Paul.

We had been modestly successful; I'd sold up my interest and rested on both my laurels and the profits for a while, mainly to play golf. Paul headed off to do other things on another continent but by now the hotelier bug had bitten me. With a new partner and brother-in-law, Ted, we looked around for a more salubrious prospect.

When they think they have a live one, estate agents are remarkably predatory and we were besieged with offers to view.

We nearly fell for one in the Lake District but fortunately could not decide. A few months later, Foot and Mouth ravaged the area and would undoubtedly have emptied the hotel and our bank account along with it. Borrowing large sums of money, as we would have had to, would almost certainly have led to us hanging ourselves from the lakeside tree, along with the local bank manager and the many unfortunate farmers.

But right down south, in the delightful county of Dorset, we felt we had found just the place. One business among the hundreds offered to us that kept being sent for consideration was Mortons House Hotel, in Corfe Castle, Dorset. Ally, my wife, (hereinafter referred to as Sybil) and I had earlier dismissed it because it was too expensive for us alone, but now, with Ted and his wife, Ally's sister Bev (Sybling), as partners, it might just be affordable. I visited after doing my homework on the Isle of Purbeck and the surrounding area. I already knew a little about Sandbanks and Brownsea Island, having spent many holidays there when I was younger. A short ferry ride connected the mainland to the peninsula or 'Isle.'

Part of the appeal of the property was its history – and also the location, as we had young families and the draw of the beaches would be difficult to resist. Coastal walks, revisiting Dancing Ledge and Lulworth Cove, or my favourite Durdle Door, would all fit rather nicely into the downtime of the potential new owners, not to mention a local golf course once owned by Enid Blyton. With four of us, one couple could be off with the five children from both families, while the other toiled and grafted. That was an early plan.

In addition, running alongside the hotel was the Swanage steam railway, and Corfe Castle station was just beyond the border wall, another popular visitor attraction. Guests in the two rooms that overlook the station can view steam trains pulling in and out with a puff of smoke and a peep from the whistle. Other rooms had views of the Castle itself.

Mortons House had been built as a country residence in 1590 for the Dackombe family, and in the shape of an 'E' - to commemorate Elizabeth I. Latterly the manor house was transferred through marriage to the Morton family. Thomas Morton married Mary Dackombe in 1633, according to the Royal Peculiar of Corfe Castle. In more recent times, the Bond family owned it. It remained a private residence until the mid-eighties when Mortons House started off as a hotel with just seven bedrooms. By the time we took over it boasted seventeen ensuite bedrooms.

We were smitten, not only by the area and surroundings but also by the magnificent view the place afforded of Corfe Castle. Probably the Dackombes considered this view of that crumbling pile as a bit of a downside, but times change and now guests clamour for the rooms with a view of the ruins.

The hotel had also a fine reputation that in turn meant that it had a fine price attached to it. You have probably noticed how bankers, when being touched for a loan, narrow their eyes and purse their lips. Well, in our case, as the touch was for around the million mark, the eyes turned into mere slits and we doubted that the lips would ever return to their natural state without Botox. But we prevailed, although the owners obstinately stuck out for their original price in spite of our best efforts.

We, along with the bank, became the proud owners of Mortons House Hotel.

We also had to make it successful.

Mrs. Inspector emerged from the cloakroom attired as if for a nuclear conflict. White cap, white overalls, white coat, surgical gloves and white hygienic shoe covers.

She looked grim and, to lighten the mood, I essayed a trifle airy badinage.

"Gosh," says I, "Our kitchens aren't that bad!"

"Young man," says she, grimly, "You would be surprised."

Brandishing her clipboard and carrying a case of equipment she headed, unbidden, toward the kitchens. I trailed after her, miserably.

"I don't need you to be present," she said, "I can manage very well, thank you."

Construing this as an order to buzz off, I duly buzzed and went in search of the paperwork that I knew would be demanded.

The paperwork that any hotelier was expected to complete daily was, even then, ridiculous but I prayed the chefs had played their part. The worst bit by far was health and safety and food hygiene. Colin and Beverley were particularly good at keeping all the risk assessments and fire records up to date, but the temperature and food handler records were for others in white coats, who used knives for work. I knew where the chefs kept these folders but rarely looked inside them. Whilst Mrs. Hitler was rattling around in the kitchens, I located all I could and acquainted myself a little with the contents, warning the breakfast chef to keep out of the way in the process.

Panic calls to Beverley, Colin and the head chef, for help went unanswered.

I found her at the kitchen door. She beckoned to me and I trailed in nervously.

Opening the door of a refrigerator, she pointed inside and said:
"What do you suppose that is?"

I peered at 'it' nervously.

"Er, it looks like a half-eaten ham sandwich."

"Precisely. It is cooked ham and uncovered butter next to raw meat. Moreover, there is a salad container immediately below. This is a direct contravention of the rules."

She wrote busily on her clipboard.

"I suggest that you find the staff member responsible and admonish them severely. This sort of breach of food hygiene laws could cost you, you know."

I refrained from telling her that I would have little difficulty in finding the culprit.

That morning, in lieu of breakfast, I had made myself a hasty sandwich. A call from reception had interrupted me after one bite and I had hastily stowed it in a handy fridge – and had promptly forgotten it. I hoped she was not proposing to match the teeth marks.

She changed back into her council officer garb and escorted me into the bar to discuss her findings. She told me it was impossible to assess the overall food score without further analysis but that we had a good system and most of what she found was in very good order. Despite these encouraging comments I was starting to show signs of my discomfort at being outside my zone of knowledge. I had no idea whether what I was saying was helping or not. She would, however, need to write to the hotel officially with reference to her findings inside the refrigerator. I toyed with the idea of offering her a drink but decided against it because she didn't look the drinking type, or the type I'd drink with. Anyway, I'd wager the caterpillar in the Lollo Rosso had more personality.

When Beverley and Colin came in, they were furious and wanted to tear into the breakfast chef or the housekeepers who had clearly messed up their very neat system, which was prominently highlighted on the door of the fridge.

"This should never have happened! The staff can all read, can't they?" They were fuming.

But it was all my fault. I had the heart – but not the balls – to tell them that I had made a ham salad sandwich for elevenses and was the culprit.

I chose instead to book myself on a refresher food hygiene

course, all part of the learning experience that comes with the territory as I moved up in the world from my first venture in the business.

"The great advantage of a hotel is that it is a refuge from home life."

George Bernard Shaw

3

The Making of Basil

Having sold my interest in my first hotel, in Crowthorne, Berkshire, we spent time at our new place in Chandlers Ford, bringing me some rest and a lot of golf. But, contrary to popular opinion, there's only so much golf you can play and I soon got bored with it and the 19th hole. Our new home was just 300 yards from Sybil's sister's house; they needed to be close after the sudden early loss of both their parents.

Encouraged by my early successes as a stand-in chef, I bought a small Italian American pizzeria in partnership with Sybling. We earned enough to keep some of our savings intact and allow for more time for me on the golf course, it was from there I often travelled the short distance to Winchester to work after my game. But 'Manhattans,' as it was called, was never likely to be a big money-spinner or a long-term investment. But I learnt how to toss pizza dough like an Italian mama.

Through this, Sybling and her husband Ted were introduced to the industry and to working with me. Surprisingly, this didn't put them off sufficiently, though. One afternoon we barbequed at their house, and after far too much Rioja, discussed the possibility of buying one big hotel together. I sold them on the fact that Dial House had been a successful first venture and that I wanted to repeat this on a bigger and more profitable scale. Sybling and I had worked closely together in the restaurant, more so after she had told the chef to leave without notice one night – so we both took over the kitchen and 'winged it' as chefs for a couple of months serving 80+ on weekend nights.

But I missed the buzz of running a proper business and serving the customers as I had at Dial House. We weren't looking for an upmarket, corporate bed-and-breakfast, though. We were looking for something special.

Soon after our properties were sold, we hocked everything and took the biggest gamble of our lives. The saga of Mortons House was about to begin.

The business had been run by David and Hilary Langford for ten years and was both profitable and busy. I was little more than ten minutes into the tour David gave me, when my mind was made up. This was a great location for us, right in the middle of Enid Blyton and Thomas Hardy country. The award-winning hotel was pretty, historic, well run, affordable (well, almost) and located perfectly for two young families to enjoy the local crabbing as I had when I first visited aged seven. The excitement was brimming inside me; all I had to do was convince the others.

My wife and Ted 'inspected' the hotel the following day, being asked by the owner to masquerade as insurance assessors. One of the unforeseen problems in buying into an operating hotel is that often it all has to be done on the quiet. If the staff get wind that there's likely to be a change of ownership, they're off like scalded cats, not a happy augury for the new owners.

Sybil and her brother-in-law loved it too and between us we convinced Sybling. We haggled over the price for days using all the negotiating experience I had gained from car sales. This was to no avail; the Langfords were particularly hard-headed and would not budge far from the asking price. As they became more stubborn, so did I and a Mexican stand-off was in the making.

Their attitude towards our negotiations and me was a little eccentric, and, given that the hotel had been on the market for nearly a year, somewhat surprising. Maybe that was a prerequisite of being an hotelier, as I had had this before with the owners of Dial House. Although Hilary didn't paint her eyebrows on with a marker pen and I bet I wouldn't find any of David's toenail clippings in the shag pile, like I had in 'Fawlty Towers' Mark I. The Langfords knew what a good opportunity the hotel was for someone with a head of steam and not full of hot air.

Finally, an offer was accepted, and I placed the potential purchase in the hands of our solicitors and approached the Bank of Scotland. I knew them both well, having used them before with Dial House. My track record was good, the business plan just altered from the successful one used before. There was no need for worry except that this time we would be borrowing a seven-figure sum, putting down a deposit of about 30%.

Ted would stay at work, allowing me to set up the company and coax the acquisition to completion. The deal fell through once as personalities started to clash, but I trod more carefully and the deal was rekindled. After our properties were sold, we all moved into my mother's two-up-two-down in Charmouth, Dorset. Nine of us were there for 13 weeks until the completion finally took place on October 25th 2000. Our collective clan of five daughters loved the beach, so much so they brought most of it home each evening, but less so the cramped sleeping arrangements.

For personal reasons, I was overjoyed that we had completed the purchase. I was proud and excited at the prospect of proving my old deputy headmaster very wrong. His words were spiteful and not meant to encourage me, but they had. I really hoped he might show up as a guest one day.

I was now Squire of the Manor, aged just 34. The potential of the business was as huge as its importance locally, and the history surrounding it.

The quality of this hotel being so much higher than I'd known was not so daunting, as that was clear beforehand. The expectations of new staff and guests I also understood. But the difference between a small corporate hotel inland and a leisure hotel within an historic building in the centre of the second most visited village in the country would be an eye-opener.

Dial House had catered largely for groups of corporate clients, few of whom would be footing the bill personally. This does make a huge difference to their attitude and I had found that, provided the bar stayed open, there were remarkably few complaints from these guests.

But with the up-market, paying the bill with their own money crowd that we were now facing, things would be very different.

David and I had planned to have a simple relaxed handover that would involve no training from them. Instead, we would rely upon the general manager, Colin Twine, and the reception manager, Beverley Bell. Both had over ten years experience of the hotel and how it had been run. They had calculated all the stock and valued it prior to our arrival. I was expected to check random items and then pay up. It all sounded delightfully simple.

Our bankers, eyes still narrowed to slits and lips pursed, and their solicitors, were very much more thorough on the day as this time we were borrowing a million plus to purchase. Our solicitors, headed by Tony Struve, tried hard to cope with all the final demands and detail required before they released funds.

The Langfords were so very relaxed, organised, and almost casual, whilst we were frenetic. We were without confirmation that the funds had arrived, so I paid for all the stock quickly to show willing. In doing so without checking it first, I was duped into buying 5000 envelopes bearing the hotel name but with the wrong website address. David's solicitor had confirmed that he foresaw no insurmountable problems, no insurmountable problems being lawyer speak for having his fingers crossed.

Day two and still the money hadn't arrived; apparently our bank's solicitor was now worried about an ownership issue pertaining to a strip of unregistered land within the grounds and was still sitting on the cash. All this coming right at the last minute was just what we didn't need.

Day three and still no money, so now I was in a blind panic, and frantic calls to and fro didn't help. Eventually, I agreed to sign an indemnity insurance policy for my bankers in case of a later dispute regarding the land, and the bank coughed up, late, but it was nearly never.

During all this time we were happily trading as if the hotel was ours and been paid for. Not once did the Langfords press us to empty our wallets or push the bank for the cash. The staff, Colin and Beverley included, seemed fine – a little miffed that they had only had a week's notice of the change in ownership and new bosses' imminent arrival, but, as I said, that's the norm in this industry.

We had to pay the Langfords some interest for 'non-completion' on time, but nothing too heavy, and they were extremely fair to allow a seemingly seamless handover. It went very well, albeit two days late; there were few shocks and we looked forward to a dizzy future in a hotel that was, it appeared, the finished product. I was very nearly finished too, as the purchasing strategy had been all mine and I was the one that would have been held responsible for the problems, despite none being my fault.

We all pitched in to the task of learning the ropes of our new baby. I was cocooned upstairs in the office with Colin. Sybil was opposite me setting up her accounting system and Ted was already busy trying to understand the 400-year-old building and all its idiosyncrasies. This left Sybling floating around looking after Ella and not much else. Ella, her youngest daughter of three, was only two and not yet at nursery.

Once the accounting system was ready, Sybil introduced the new daily banking routine to the reception staff. Unfortunately, the reception manager was off duty that day. Another receptionist tried and failed to explain how easy it was. When my wife failed to convince our full-time reception manager of the system's virtues, we feared the worst.

She quit.

Doing 42 hours a week spread over six days meant that she was a linchpin. Her hours had dovetailed with Colin's, allowing the Langfords to leave the hotel to run itself under their guidance. Giving us notice so soon after we took over was a blow, but we would have to cope.

A worthwhile role for my sister-in-law had now opened up and she grasped it with both hands. We were now all properly involved by the time the village was illuminated by a million fairy lights.

Christmas was a great success as far as both the hotel and bank balance was concerned, the place was heaving, as were those who had overindulged. I was sure that it would be an eventful New Year. It certainly proved to be.

As we sang "Auld Lang Syne" with the guests in the village square, I proposed a holiday. We would all take a break for fourteen days at the beginning of the coming week, once our guests had left complete with their new resolutions. The stress of the takeover, staff losses and the sheer weight of business was something we had underestimated. I had been in the throes of finding and setting up the business for almost a year and needed to relax. There was money in the bank and Colin would cope. The business in the first two weeks of the year was minimal. Unlike us in Lanzarote, most people were dieting or on a detox.

Little did I suspect that the coming year would be our Annus Horribilis.

And little did I know what a pain in the arse the coming year would be for me – literally!

4.

Annus Horribilis

All men, great, good or otherwise seem to have had a bad year at one time or another. Napoleon had several, starting with 1812, and Adolf Hitler had a particularly disastrous one in 1945. But then, like Basil, I shouldn't mention the war.

For me, it was the first full year at Morton's House that was to be the testing time. We had got off to a 'flyer' and the bank balance was already healthy, the mortgage, staff and suppliers were paid up to date, so all was well. Owner-managed hotels like ours are often better received by the guests, as the extra attention to detail and in our case, the personalities of one Basil, his Sybil, and her Sybling to make the stay a special experience. Perhaps, regrettably, we had no Manuel on hand to provide light entertainment but Ted was as funny and equally short. Certainly the efforts we put in seemed to be working wonders with the amount of tips left for the staff to share out twice a year.

It started with a touch of low comedy on the morning after we had returned from Lanzarote. I was lying in bed, contemplating, as so many do, that, after a jolly good holiday, what one needs is a jolly good holiday to get over it, when the phone rang.

"Basil, je nai pas de chef pour les petits-dejeuners!" which I took to mean we were in the shit, because I am not used to being woken by the emergency phone by my bed, it was one of our French chef de rang, or a waiter in Basil speak.

25

Another Gallic employee, a chef, and our number two in the kitchen, was AWOL and hadn't turned up for the breakfast shift, ominously he was nicknamed 'Oily' as he was always well lubricated. We had thirty guests who would soon be down clamouring for food - and no chef.

At times like these one has to admire the continental Europeans. Give them a demi-tasse of coffee and croissant filled with chocolate and they might go quietly. But Brits are made of sterner stuff and demand their ration of pig and hen fruit in order to get the day off to a good start.

In a trice I was at my post in the kitchen, demonstrating my qualities of leadership, and had the nosh on the go in no time. The pork and leek sausages were just coming into their prime when in walks Oily.

Only he didn't walk in, he reeled in, fending himself off one of the refrigerators en route. He seemed surprised to find me at the helm of what he regarded as his ship and more than little bit miffed about it. He appeared to have been celebrating something a little too well and certainly very unwisely as his eyes were as red as the grilling tomatoes, and I was fearful that his breath might get near a naked flame.

We wrestled over a spatula as he tried to take over the sausage cooking and, as diplomatically as I could, I suggested that he should go home to lie down to sleep it off. This seemed to have struck some Gallic nerve. Did I think he was incapable? Yes, he was late but he was here now, wasn't he? De Gaulle must have felt the same way when they forgot to tell him about D-Day.

As he staggered and swayed, he mistook the stress that showed on my face as the orders started to flow in to mean he was at fault in some way, or indeed in trouble. I later learned that he cooked best when like this; I just hadn't seen it before now or he would have worked his last shift for us long ago.

I asked him to leave the kitchen, but when he refused I 'led' him from the kitchen with his arms behind his back. He threatened to kill me with a plastic spatula, not now maybe, given where his arms were, but some time in the future when I was not looking. Welcome back, boss.

So for the next few mornings I was on duty until we could find a replacement. My kitchen shifts started to become easier and service was as well oiled as the departed chef.

It will probably have occurred to you that running a hotel would be pretty easy were it not for two things. The guests and the staff. And any accountant with a sharp pencil will point out that, whilst the absence of these will undoubtedly make life a lot easier, it's not likely to be much of a commercial success.

But once in a while, a guest will become such a pain that the only thing to do is to dispense with their custom. And so it was with the Olivers.

Six months before we took over our Elizabethan manor, Mr. Oliver and his wife celebrated his seventieth birthday by inviting guests to a good-sized function. Due to its success, they returned alone, to again enjoy the comforts on offer, only to find new owners at the helm of the Elizabethan manor.

As they had stayed at the hotel before, they knew their way around and seemed happy enough during their two night 'Hibernation Break', which includes dinner as part of the package. On the second evening, however, I was called into the restaurant by Colin, who was running the show that night. He explained that there was a problem with Mr. Oliver at Table 7.

I approached, confident that I could deal with anything.

"Since you took over, the service has dropped dramatically and we are not happy," he said, a good deal louder than necessary.

"Really? I'm sorry to hear that. But in what way?"

He went on to explain that his experience the previous night had just been repeated and this was grounds for complaint.

"Other tables have been served before us," he complained, fortissimo, "yet we have been sitting here longer than them."

Patiently I reminded him that we invite guests to come down a bit earlier than the time booked for dinner so that they can enjoy the complimentary canapés and a pre-dinner drink in the drawing room. This information is relayed to every guest at check-in. I enlarged upon the comfort and convenience of this arrangement, the luxury of the oak panelled walls, the exotic carvings by Indonesian sailors and the huge log fire not to mention the three different gins on offer behind the bar. At this point, we present menus whilst the guests take their ease on our comfortable furniture and we later take their order. When the chefs are prepared to serve the first course, we invite the guests into the restaurant. It works like clockwork, is customary in English country hotels and avoids the delay that normally occurs before the first course.

But there's always one in every pack and he and his wife had chosen to ignore this and wander straight into the dining room each night and, without waiting to be seated, settled themselves at a table. Perhaps they had an aversion to carvings by Indonesian sailors, I suppose some might as they are a bit saucy, but whatever the cause, they had skipped a vital part of the script.

Clearly, those being seated around them in the restaurant were going to be served first, as they had ordered up to 30 minutes earlier.

It all seemed pretty reasonable to me but not to the Olivers whose complaints were getting louder and louder, probably much to the amusement of the surrounding tables but not to me. I could feel my first funny walk coming on. We had a heated debate about my system, but with each syllable he used, he got more and more vehement.

"So I am being victimised for not being an alcoholic!"

Having been weaned in negotiation by the motor trade, I had to think quickly and on my feet to avoid more disturbance and unease or maybe amusement amongst other guests in our rather busy restaurant.

An idea came to me in a flash. "Mr Oliver, rather than debate this any further, why don't I change your booking from an inclusive dinner, bed and breakfast tariff, to our bed and breakfast rate? Then you will not have paid for any of your meals!" He looked very pleased, and he even thanked me. Problem solved, I thought.

Our table d'hôte menu was priced at £24 per head to guests on B&B or non-residents. However, if you chose to stay two nights on a half-board basis, dinner was included. The rate for this was £55.50 per person per night. The bed and breakfast rate was £50 per person per night. The reason for the minimal difference was to encourage guests to spend two nights and eat both nights with us. It keeps the chefs and waiting staff employed twelve months a year.

On checkout the following morning, I heard a shriek of "You must be joking!" from reception. I knew that Mr. Oliver was ready to leave and so I went to savour the moment. The red-faced customer greeted me almost before I got to the desk.

He was waving the bill at me like he was in Parliament and looked on the verge of apoplexy. I explained that he had indeed been charged for B&B and no food was on his bill; unfortunately he was expecting a reduction of £24 per person per night, being the cost of the menu, saving him nearly one hundred pounds. I had calculated that his total saving was around £20: a clever piece of negotiation and one that was entirely correct, as he had only paid for his room and breakfast. Mr Oliver was getting vocal again, so I guided him and his wife into the drawing room they'd ignored the night before, to discuss the issues he clearly had.

The final straw was his comment that the food was so perfectly displayed on the plate that he could only imagine this possible if the food was frozen and micro-waved in situ before serving.

Now, complaining about the service might have been one thing but to cast aspersions on the chef and the food standards was another, his condescending tone had gotten to me. So now I truly had a full head of steam and was ready to let some off. I could sense my nostrils flaring, almost 'Basil-esque'. I knew that, for the first time in my professional life, I was about to give a paying customer the middle finger. I just couldn't stop myself.

I told the Olivers that I would alter their invoice to the amount that their business was worth to me. I went to reception and asked them to produce an invoice for one penny. I returned to the Oak Room and presented the new bill. A shocked Mr. Oliver looked blankly at it, said not a word but then commented that he'd expect a letter from the hotel's solicitor at a later date, chasing the balance of their bill.

"On the contrary," I said, taking a single copper penny from my pocket and giving it to him. "If you take this penny to the reception desk and settle your bill, I will sign it as 'paid in full'."

The couple left the hotel into the cold February morning, the frost breaking under their feet. After they had loaded their old looking Austin Montego, they prepared to leave. Unfortunately, the car wouldn't start, as the battery was clearly not up to the job of jolting the frozen old car into action. When a forlorn Mr. Oliver returned to reception, I was waiting for him with a similarly sarcastic smile to the one he had shown me earlier.

"Do you have any jump leads I could borrow?" he asked, sheepishly. "My car has a flat battery."

"But of course, Mr. Oliver, we hire them to guests for £238.20." This being the amount of his original unaltered bill.

He decided to go into the village to find some jump leads. I told him he was welcome to do so, but I had to warn him that the hotel operated a very strict 'clamping policy' for non-resident cars parked in the car park.

"But I am a guest!" he shrieked, the apoplexy returning with a vengeance.

"No, Mr. Oliver," I replied, glibly, "guests normally pay and besides, you have already checked out!"

Strange that he hasn't been back.

Basil had put his first guest to the sword.

It wasn't a good start to the year. Turning profitable business away, for whatever reason, never is but I did feel a warm glow of satisfaction, as I believe that Mr. Oliver got his just desserts. Never try and bully your innkeeper especially when he happens to be me!

But barely had the Olivers chugged out of our car park than another problem guest showed up. Or, more precisely, didn't show up.

Foot and Mouth disease was affecting many areas of the country and, as a precaution, there was an embargo on walking dogs almost anywhere in the region. We had taken a booking from a Mr. Perker and party, which was to include their three dogs, at the beginning of the farmers' woes, for three rooms for three days, on a dinner, bed and breakfast tariff. The party would arrive with their pets. At the time the hotel accepted dogs, and so this seemed like a good booking that Sybling had taken. It was guaranteed by credit card.

Whilst personally I didn't have foot and mouth, I did have a very painful ear infection at the time and hence my mood was, if anything, a little less tranquil than usual, which means that the barometer was set to 'stormy.'

On the Thursday in February 2001 when we'd expected the Perker party, the hotel was all but full; in fact Friday and Saturday were full. The day came and went with no sign of him or his party, so we called the number he'd given. There was no reply, but an answering machine accepted our message. We repeated this several times over the following days, asking about his intentions, but heard nothing.

The hotel operates a very strict cancellation and 'No Show' policy, which I drew up after some bad experiences at the Dial House, which included a dead man checking in a week after his wife cancelled a booking because he had died. This was quoted to all guests, and goes like this: "The hotel's cancellation policy is seven days prior to the date of arrival for any part of the booking. In the event of late cancellation or 'No Show', the hotel charges in all cases. If you think it is possible or likely you may cancel within this time, we recommend you take out appropriate travel insurance." We do go on to say that we charge 75% of the total booking value. There is a booking card that prompts all reception staff to ask ALL the questions when taking a booking. As in this case, we take a credit card number, expiry date and so on, to guarantee the booking.

The following Monday morning, Mr. Perker rang the hotel to explain that he'd cancelled his reservation by fax. We asked him to send us a copy, and he did so five minutes later; but what came out at our end was not what we expected. The fax did indeed confirm his cancellation, but was addressed and sent to The Manor House Hotel, a competitor of ours with the same telephone area code. As we always give a 'cancellation reference' before we remove a booking and there wasn't one for this booking, I wasn't surprised.

Presumably they were savouring this at the Manor House since they didn't bother to forward the fax to us although it was clearly sent to them in error.

I called Mr. Perker to explain the situation, and also to clarify what charges we had made to the credit card he gave as guarantee. This was done in three increments, on each of the days his party failed to show up. The first was for 75% of the total booking for the Thursday night, of £282.75. The Friday was a more expensive rate and totalled £318, the same for the Saturday. The total debited was over £900.

Mr. Perker was understandably distressed but didn't protest. He was clearly in the wrong and not only knew it but appeared to understand. He would have loved to have come to my hotel, but with the restrictions on dog walking due to Foot and Mouth disease, he couldn't justify coming to Dorset. All very reasonable, I thought.

The next day he called and asked me to make a gesture of goodwill in his favour. But as we had only been in business for a few months, every penny counted. His story was a bit different, and I was feeling a bit guilty for the losses made on the Oliver saga, so unusually I consulted partners Sybling and Ted to gauge their thoughts. We decided to offer a refund of one of the nights. I did this by letter to Mr. Perker, stating clearly that the offer was non-negotiable and done only as gesture of good will – not something for which I was becoming renowned. As the hotel wasn't full on the first night of his 'No Show', it was this cancellation fee I offered to refund him, £282.75.

Mr. Perker's letter arrived a few days later, stating that he thought I was being most unfair to offer him a refund of the least expensive night's cancellation fee, going on to mention that I could have resold the rooms to reduce the amount he'd be liable for. Because of the tone of his letter and because he had the audacity to try and negotiate, I wrote back to him retracting my kind offer; the full cancellation charge would stand. There was now a bad case of 'Basil' breaking out in Corfe Castle too.

A number of very boring and irrelevant letters ensued, until I got one that said "I'll see you in court." My wife and my partners all felt that I should back down and save time, but I wanted to test my cancellation policy. If that meant court, so be it. I might have changed my mind many times during the paperwork submission to the courts, though. I requested the hearing in Bournemouth and waited.

Being in limbo awaiting a court case is not much fun. But I soon had other problems to deal with.

There isn't a good quality hotel in the world that accepts dogs, other than those that guide the blind. But I was told that my hotel was in the centre of the coastal walking capital of England and that taking dogs was apparently vital to our business. We decided to honour bookings taken before we had arrived and review the situation later in the spring if the furniture hadn't been chewed to death in the meantime.

It was a close run thing.

Events early in the spring involving canine guests would make me clarify our views earlier than expected. One of many incidents was with a regular guest, Mr. Johnson. He always came without his wife, but with Tiny, his Great Dane, who I can only assume was better company or maybe better looking.

After dinner he'd always walk the mutt before sitting in front of the fire to smoke a pipe. One night when he did this, all the fireplace seats in the oak-panelled drawing room were taken. As I was following him in with his Cognac and Petit Fours, I saw him encourage Tiny to the fire, not seen by the couple occupying 'his' seat. Tiny took his cue and went straight to the fire, pausing, before he sat down across the full length of the Minster fireplace, to sniff the crotch of the woman sitting there.

Certain breeds of dogs are admirably designed for this purpose. Rarely do you see a Pekingese or Chihuahua performing this trick unless they have a box to stand on. But Great Danes are ideally designed for the job. That may have been enough, but then to sneeze on the poor woman post-sniff seemed too much. She went ballistic, to the amusement of Mr. Johnson and the shock of everyone else, including the dog, who probably swore to give up crotch-sniffing for evermore.

The woman, it turned out had a canine phobia, and had never been confronted by anything like it before. She was a wreck and quickly afterwards checked out, but not before recounting to the receptionist the full details of Tiny sniffing her Foo Foo. The guest left in tears, and now the receptionist was in tears too, whether because hers hadn't been sniffed or not, I don't know.

But the final straw came with Mrs. Bardell, who arrived with her King Charles Spaniels and checked into a recently redecorated character room in the old part of the building. When Mrs. Bardell dined in the restaurant, the three spaniels went mad, with howling and non-stop barking of an almost hysterical nature. It was upsetting the neighbouring rooms and those just downstairs in the bar and the Oak Room. I begged Mrs. Bardell repeatedly during her meal to do something about it. Finally, she left the dining room and went to her bedroom. When she came out, she was as white as a sheet – not the bright red face of the furious woman who had been disturbed during her dinner and escorted in by me minutes earlier.

"Do you have ghosts?" she questioned.

"Er, no, madam, not that I am aware of," I lied.

She explained that she had felt a cold presence in the room and something brush her face. The dogs were never, ever hysterical – something that could not be said of me once I had seen the bedroom. In fact, the dogs had trashed the room, torn all the fabric on the new tapestry throw, and left pee and poo all over the place. Clearly not their fault, Mrs. Bardell insisted, but the ghost's.

It was touch and go whether we should ban dogs or ghosts in the future, but as there had been stories of ghosts in the house for many years, we decided to let them stay.

Consequently, there would be no more dogs at the hotel. We cancelled all remaining bookings with canine guests and redecorated the room once again.

It wasn't the first time that guests had reported ghosts – certainly not in Room 2, where she and her dogs had stayed. One friend of mine said he'd awoken in the night to see a woman sitting on the end of his bed, as clear as crystal, watching him. To hear this from a 20+ stone rugby playing, no-nonsense type of chap was a surprise, as he wasn't the type to tell such tales or give any credence to others that did.

"My hand passed right through her when I made a grab at her," he told me. I told him that I had often had similar experiences when I made a grab for an attractive girl but he insisted that this one had been a ghost.

I was recalling these stories in the bar to a very interested regular, Mrs. Binnwicky. She loves her double G&T's and is always asking me to recall the latest intended chapter of my 'never-to-be-written book' to her and her party. I told it with great passion, and in great detail, leading them out of the bar to the staircase to Room 2 just above. When I got to the bit where I dismissed ghosts as rubbish and had ignored Mrs. Bardell's protestations that her hounds had nothing to do with it, the door to Room 2 slammed shut and a huge piece of decorative coving beneath the room crashed to the floor.

I gave serious thought to lifting the ban on dogs. I might have done them an injustice, I felt. I no longer recount stories of things that go bump in the night in case 'they' are listening. Although guests still ask about hearing a crying baby in Room 1, even when it is empty.

Spring moved towards summer, and like many families with young children we started to enjoy the area. Having children at the hotel was almost a rarity outside of the school holidays, and under-fives were not allowed to dine in the restaurant in the evenings. The area has much to offer, so we usually only saw kids at breakfast and at high tea.

Early evening was the time we fed the Koi carp in the pond. Children were encouraged by their beautiful colours and enjoyed this time. A few dozen large Koi and at least double that amount of goldfish take a while to feed. The pond is about 30 feet long and deceptively deep in the middle.

At feeding time, the fish surface and almost thrash around in anticipation. If you gently ripple the pond with your fingers before feeding, the carp will literally rise and suck them. I enjoyed demonstrating this every night, often giving an ankle biter the opportunity to distribute the food afterwards.

One summer's evening, we had a family staying at the hotel for a break. The children, Josh, 7, Jack, 5 and Rosie, 3, were the perfect age to enjoy the steam railway, beaches and castle, if not the coastal walks their parents loved. They were ever-present at feeding time at the pond, this being the final treat of their day. They knew the routine and were marshalled by me while the parents sat close by, drinking Pimms. After the fish had been fed, I had to return to my duties serving the pre-dinner drinks to the guests with stories and anecdotes. The host was full on for those that enjoyed it and mindful of the others. I left the young family together by the pond.

It wasn't a very busy night, but it would help pay the wages and keep Sybil in shoes. I had time whilst serving drinks to see the boys outside jumping the width of the pond. I went out to warn them that it was dangerous and might scare the fish, so I asked them to refrain. Inevitably, only a few minutes later I heard a scream and a splash, followed by shouting and another splash. I didn't need to guess. Josh was up to his neck in water and Jack out of his depth, trying to reach the side. Rosie helped and was dragged in too.

The parents flapped around and did little to help. Dressed in one of my better suits and favourite tie, I jumped in and gathered the youngest children by the scruffs of their necks and deposited them on the flagstone pond side. Josh made his own way out of the pond.

As the kids coughed and spluttered, their parents turned on me, screaming their claim that I had taken responsibility for them and that I had left the children unattended after feeding the fish with them. They also made out that they were oblivious to my warnings about the danger of jumping the pond and that I had left the kids in order to carry out my restaurant work.

Hell hath no fury like parents who know they have failed to take care of their offspring and are looking around for someone to blame.

The water from the pond is filtered, but after three kids had thrashed around for a while it was murky and green. The sludge from its depths was now floating to the surface of the pond and out of my handmade Loakes. Josh and Rosie were sick by the pond side. Clearly they had all gulped plenty. The parents asked me to call a doctor for advice on any treatment necessary. The out-of-hours doctor suggested going to Poole Hospital accident and emergency department for stomach pumping – after all, fish shit and make more little fishes in water.

The family disappeared for the casualty department, leaving behind them threats and insults. I ran to the cottage to change, doing so in such quick time, with no explanation to the amazed co-owners watching soap operas in front of the television and log fire, that I returned to work within minutes. I was wishing that I could stay with them enjoying a glass of red wine from the hotel wine list. Thankfully the evening passed without further problems or disturbances. My guests reassured the worried host that I had not been at fault. But what if the children were really ill, I wondered.

At check-out the following day, the accusations and threats continued to come my way from the parents of the sick-looking children. They had returned at midnight with empty tummies. I protested my innocence, but they assured me that I would hear from their solicitors and no doubt, the Health and Safety officer. In these days of litigation I was not confident that I wouldn't meet the lady inspector in the white coat again, sometime soon. Colleagues and advisors tried to calm my fears that I wouldn't have to put up with another visit from the Environmental Health Department.

To my relief I heard nothing. I was very much more careful not to appear to take supervision of children again. I cannot stop them being fascinated by the fish, though, and I do make more of the dangers now.

These excitements had temporarily driven the impending court case from my mind but in the early autumn I had received confirmation from Aylesbury County Court that the case with Mr. Perker would be heard there.

As a private individual brought the action against my Limited Company, he, the claimant, could choose the venue.

Even though I drove to the court alone, and without a solicitor I felt ready. I had all the documents, and had sent copies to both the court and Mr. Perker. The waiting room was filled with a veritable plethora of society, but there was one gentleman, kind of 'country-looking,' who was my opponent.

Judge Owen heard from Mr. Perker first. He said nothing new, but significantly, when asked about whether the hotel's cancellation policy was quoted to him, he said he couldn't remember. His evidence took around 35 minutes to hear.

Then Judge Owen turned to me. I was set and primed. I went straight into the fact that the booking was guaranteed and the dictionary states that this word means 'outcome certain.' The guarantee was further reinforced by the credit card with its expiry date, willingly given. My final point was that the hotel had no way to mitigate its loss, because we couldn't re-let the rooms, not having received a cancellation. We would, however, have been liable for the costs of alternative accommodation for him and his party if we had sold his rooms and Mr. Perker had turned up a day late.

I treated this date in court as one more performance, enjoying every moment. I had a case and was busy proving it. Unfortunately, Judge Owen interrupted me repeatedly by asking in-depth and detailed questions. Clearly, he wasn't responding well to my performance. Things were looking bad. I started to wonder whether I'd need the single company cheque I'd brought with me. Confidence is one thing; considering these facts, I thought it justified. But every one of these small claims can go either way. It's the opinion and decision of only one person, the judge.

In his summing up, Judge Owen clearly sympathised with Mr. Perker. He made use of every one of his claims to make mine seem less plausible. Could my day in court really go as badly wrong as it was beginning to look?

In summary, the judge said: "In conclusion, I feel the hotel had no opportunity to mitigate its losses and in all probability quoted to the claimant the terms of its cancellation policy before the contract was made. The hotel's charges reflect exactly the terms set out in that policy. Therefore I find in favour of the plaintiff."

I was sure I was the 'plaintiff' – wasn't I? The face of Mr. Perker confirmed this view. As we left chambers together and headed towards the lifts, he said: "I suppose fairness is not an option here: it just comes down to the law."

I didn't say a word, but couldn't help myself from thinking that this was the whole point of his bringing me here, and what did he expect? The journey home was through torrential rain, but I had had a great, winning day, and didn't care.

It was one bright spot in an otherwise stressful year. Our first had been very busy and successful but equally hard on me - although there were some lighter moments.

That autumn, we had an extremely cold spell, before the chimney had been swept. I took a risk and lit the fire in the Oak Room. Soon afterwards, a telltale roar from above confirmed that we had a chimney fire. The sticks from crows nesting earlier that year and last year's soot were alight, a danger to the building and its guests. There was no way we could extinguish the fire on our own, least of all one halfway up the sixty-foot chimney stack. So I called the fire brigade.

Soon the blues and twos of the fire engines filled the rain-soaked car park of the hotel. The fire brigade had a plan of the hotel and immediately asked if they could get access to the loft space above the honeymoon suite.

A couple had checked into this suite an hour earlier greeted by a chilled bottle of bubbly, the woman was celebrating her fortieth birthday in our best room. Our problem was that there was no answer from the room telephone; presumably they were busy at the time.

The lads from the fire brigade joked as to why, but the officer with the white helmet was not for wasting any more time. He despatched four men to inspect the roof void via the loft hatch located in the bathroom. After letting them into the room, it was apparent that the couple were enjoying a Jacuzzi. The 'gentleman' came out and laughed when he saw the fire brigade, then ushered them into the bathroom. I didn't follow them in, but apparently the lady was now somewhat giggly and was happy to allow the strapping chaps in to climb up the ladder to get a better view of her in the Spa bath – she even egged them on to strip off for her.

Her husband told me that she loved anything in a uniform and would enjoy this no end. In the end, the chimney fire was dealt with from the Oak Room, much to the disappointment of the couple whose Jacuzzi had been interrupted.

It was only the following morning that all became clear. The couple that had been disturbed mid-Jacuzzi had thought it was a wind-up to help her celebrate her big 4-0. They thought their mischievous mates had paid for the chaps 'from the fire brigade' to attend. The birthday girl who'd shown off her birthday suit was mortified when the guys didn't strip off; but when she realised the truth she went a whiter shade of pale. She hit her husband for laughing like a hyena, and for letting them all in to the bathroom.

She wrote to me later though, and clearly now saw the funny side, as did all the guys from Swanage Fire Station to whom I forwarded her letter. They're looking forward to our giving them more business.

The winter months always made the Oak Room more popular, especially with the fire lit. The drawing room contains many high backed Knoll settees and is where most guests retire to after dinner. The more romantic couples that leave the restaurant often get hidden behind those settees that are wall facing for extra privacy.

One night, when I thought that everyone had retired to bed, I was clearing the coffee cups and ashtrays and was sure that I heard a noise from the far corner of the room. I walked towards the noise and saw a shoe on the floor, female type. Thinking it would add to the lost property collection, I went to retrieve it. As I got closer, I discovered bodies, closely intertwined. Partially dressed and clearly not noticing me as they continued to make love. Marvellous for them that they felt so much at home, but why not use the bedroom they had booked? Neither appeared to notice me, but just as I turned to leave, the lady panted, "Rather than just stand there gawping, could you get me some water please?"

I didn't know what to say or do, so I fetched her some water like an obedient host should. But when I returned I was amazed when they didn't stop the performance for her to drink it, she handed me back the empty glass whilst still gasping, but not for more water!

The darker months are also quieter during the daytime, so we need fewer staff on duty. But as the rain poured down one afternoon, the hotel started to get busy with non-residents wanting shelter and a cream tea.

Two lads walked in wanting only to use the toilet, which we do not allow, as there is a public convenience in the village centre, but they used the toilets anyway and were asked to leave by the duty manager.

The lads had clearly cased the hotel before leaving, and they came back later during a busier moment. Opposite the gents' toilets is a payphone, which we had not emptied all year, thinking that this was something BT did for us. The lads simply came back, ripped the whole thing out, placed it in a holdall and went up the fire escape next to the ladies' loo. They then came down the main staircase and walked out the front door, which is something the receptionist saw often. But she failed to notice these two juveniles wearing 'hoodies' carrying a bag rattling with coins in a box.

The new payphone is in the same location but is now screwed to the wall and alarmed. We also empty it once a week, taking out the £10 or so in change that is so useful for the bar till.

We lost £400 on the payphone and, on the basis of receipts since, approximately £500 on its contents.

The only other moneybox onsite was located within a pair of Labradors at the front door. These collected for the Guide Dogs for the Blind and were now the only dogs allowed on the premises.

Even though the reception staff weren't too busy to notice the two yobs run in, they were too slow to stop them grabbing the plastic dogs and taking them for a run along East Street, when they were also spotted by villagers.

The empty box was found on the village green. Sad, really, that they chose a charitable target; sad, too, that the thieves couldn't be identified by anybody that saw them. Without any clues the police never had a chance and there weren't any arrests. We sent a generous contribution to the charity and have another pair of guide dogs guarding the door. They are now chained to the wall, too.

But of all the trials and tribulations of the year, the most saddening for me occurred early, soon after we had taken over.

My parents until then had only seen the hotel in print, and I had invited them to see their youngest son's latest venture, and newest pride and joy. My father had driven his ex-wife (my mother, Julia) from her home in Charmouth. He visited her regularly and they remained good friends. They arrived early one morning after a heavy frost. I had a very long day ahead, having planned to show them around the hotel in the morning, followed by a light lunch. Pop would prefer to drive Ma home before it got dark. My afternoon would be taken up with paperwork and planning the busy evening dinner service.

I wanted to get started on the tour, but neither of my parents seemed keen to leave the warmth of the cottage and the conversation with Sybil and Sybling. Once I insisted, they reluctantly followed me up the steps towards the hotel. My mother was more agile and kept up with my rush-rush, busy-busy, rush-rush attitude. My father lagged behind after only a few paces. The next few steps he took started the terminal decline in his health. Trying to walk at my speed, he trod on the edge of one step. The frost had weakened the mortar and it gave way under his weight.

The first I knew was the groan of pain as he fell. Tour over. I took him to Dorchester emergency department. His injuries were described as minimal, and he was discharged. Nobody noticed the ruptured bicep and nerve damage among the broken ribs and general soreness.

I was so looking forward to showing them around the manor as the new squire. Mum got her tour later. But my father never got another chance.

To top off all my troubles that first year I was left with an embarrassing and uncomfortable condition. I thought I had piles. As it was not something I had suffered from before, I attended the local doctor's surgery for confirmation and hopefully remedy, as walking, indeed sitting down, had become very painful.

As I was called into the examination room, my heart sank. Instead of my regular doctor there was a locum on duty, and, worse, it was a woman. Explaining how hard it had become to walk, work or sit with my condition, the doctor wasted no time and asked me to show her the problem. I am uncomfortable showing my arse to anyone, let alone a female doctor, but bend down I did. I knew that if it looked as bad as it felt then it wasn't going to be a pretty sight; indeed, she winced almost as much as I did when sitting back down.

There are few quick solutions to piles, the doctor told me, but she prescribed some cream that I would have to apply. I told her that I was likely to be unable to work unless the relief was fast. Just as I was leaving her office she made another suggestion. If the pain was too much to bear, she told me that I could always fill a condom with ice cubes, tie a knot in the end and insert this up the affected area.

I was not overly keen to put a condom up my arse, especially if filled with something, but as I was willing to try anything, I did as I was told. The problem was that once I had inserted the relief, it was impossible to move to and lie on my bed. The slightest movement, laughter or frustration was enough to make me to involuntarily expel the condom, and the position I had to get into to insert

44

the thing wasn't easy to do in situ. My wife Sybil was in hysterics, which added greatly to my embarrassment – in sickness and in hysterics would have been a better marriage vow.

Finally, I managed to get everything in place and waddle penguin-like to the bed. All I needed to do now was get into a lying position. In an attempt to get horizontal, I half hopped and half fell on the bed, my 'Fosbury flop' sent the condom from my bum like a rocket. The speed and distance the ice-filled rubber travelled across the bedroom floor astonished us both and had us in stitches of laughter. The last try was the most dramatic and the funniest.

But it was the doctor's diagnosis that summed up my whole year pretty well.

She had said my anus was indeed horrible!

But time is a great healer and once in a while there comes a light-hearted incident to brighten your day – or in this case, several people's nights.

"St. Teresa of Avila described our life in this world as like a night at a second-class hotel."

Malcolm Muggeridge

5

The Sleepwalker

G ood morning, I am sorry to bother you, but I have locked myself out of my room. Incidentally, perhaps I should also point out that I have no clothes on."

The phone next to my bed in the cottage across the car park from the hotel should never have rung at all. I was manning the night phones purely because staff had let me down. The switchboard at the hotel was set to ring by my bedside should there be a night time emergency. Standing naked in the middle of a hotel reception in the dead of night was no such thing, for me anyway. The guy clasping his credentials without a stitch on clearly thought differently.

It was 3.45am and it had taken some ringing to wake me after a very long day during my annus horribilis. I decided that with my Hugh Heffner style dressing gown and the slippers that would match my hastily thrown on jeans, there was no time for knickers. Now that was more like the Playboy founder, I thought.

As I trudged across the frosted gravel car park towards the hotel I made plenty of noise. The idea of having gravel is for exactly this reason; staff and receptionists can hear guests coming. Only this time I was trying to be as quiet as a creeping mouse. But I was sure my naked guest knew I was on my way.

As I keyed in the code at the front door to enter the reception area I could see the shape of my now freezing streaker silhouetted by the night-light. Holding his testicles one minute then offering to shake my hand the next, during our first introduction was too much, too soon. But as not many streakers introduce themselves, things were looking up I thought. The real problem now was that he was a guest but had no idea which room he was from. During the time it took me to find the reception desk key from a bunch a size fit for a jailer, I had learnt that the guy was a sleepwalker.

We were now both awake, me trying to locate him in the reservation book and him talking too loud with profuse apologies. Finally I found his room, booked in the name of his partner and I assumed she would be asleep upstairs as I should have been, in the cottage.

I led 'Steve' to room 12, on the way thinking how weird it was to be followed down a long hotel corridor by a naked man in his twenties. On reaching his room I knocked at the door. And knocked again a moment later. Then I tried the door handle to find the door was locked. The door next to it opened and a surprised looking elderly gentleman laughed at what he saw in the corridor.

"What's going on here then?" he chuckled. I tried to explain but to no avail, but thankfully he retreated, laughing heartily. From the jailers bunch of keys I found one for the housekeeping cupboard and obtained the spare key to 'Steve's' room.

Just as I unlocked it I heard his partner call out from within and I was a bit shocked but too tired to care when what I heard wasn't 'Steve.' But when the door opened they seemed to recognise each other so I could relax a bit. 'Steve' outstretched a hand of thanks, but given its proximity to his balls for the last twenty minutes I declined again.

I ventured across the gravel again, this time, with a crunch too many for the guests in room 2. They turned on their bedroom light and peered out at the innkeeper in disguise, retreating home to Sybil.

She didn't say much, except to question why the telephone system had rung us and not the live-in staff, whose duties would include this sort of event. But we had no reliable English speakers in the staff accommodation that night and it seemed the sensible thing to do, after all the fire alarms had to be manned, I told her confidently. Sybil didn't remove her eye mask to interrogate me further about my nocturnal jaunt. She employs this to shut out any light and enable her to slumber. I might have copped a lot less of an eyeful of 'Steve's' tackle, when he removed his hand to shake mine if I had borrowed it I thought before slipping under the duvet to warm my frozen toes on her legs.

At breakfast there was no sign of the couple staying in room 12 in the dining room. I did see the old buffer in room 11 again, though, he teased me about what Basil and the guests get up to in the dark of the night, a little louder than I would have wanted, right in the middle of the restaurant. I tried a little harder than I had the previous night to explain what had happened but I didn't want to make 'Steve's' entrance at breakfast any harder, so the information I gave was a little sketchy, then again that was all I had. I figured it unlikely that the old fella was a psychiatrist, but like the one in Torquay, this would be book worthy.

By now the receptionist had found the sleepwalkers room key. It was in the Oak Room waste bin. 'Steve' had apparently left the room 'asleep' locked the door and wandered around the ground floor until waking up confused. He then woke the even more confused Basil. I could not understand the night before how he had locked himself out, as he needed the key to lock the door?

When 'Steve' and his partner came down long after breakfast had finished, too embarrassed to have a Purbeck Grill, I heard their story and the history of the sleepwalker. I advised them to lock the bedroom door from the inside and take out the key so that he couldn't get out for a nocturnal wander. They had another night to stay in the Elizabethan manor.

The day passed without great event, except the verbal jibes from

49

the 'psychiatrist' it was a peaceful day. The hotel and I had a decent evening, 34 diners ate the fare produced by the men in white coats and had received some great punter reviews. These reviews are rarely passed on to the madmen of the snake pit because that would fuel their egos, generally I translate a customers "fabulous" into Basil's "barely adequate." I did my rounds of the Oak Room and restaurant before heading home across the gravel for some essential sleep after a busy day.

"There is a man in our bed! Please come and help us!" The phone by my bed had rung at 4.00am; Sybil was less than amused to be woken again. I had transferred the phones to the cottage because the member of staff who let me down the night before had borne the brunt of the sleepwalker's antics and Sybil's mood and had left my employ.

The couple that called me were in room 10. I knew this because their name and room number were displayed on my phone when I answered the distress call. When I reached the room there was a 'welcome' committee. The couple in room 10 were outside it talking to the 'psychiatrist' from next door.

"He's in there!" said the woman who had more men in her bed than she wanted, and who was now visibly shaking.

"What happened?" was the only sensible question I could muster whilst noticing the psychiatrist eyeing my Playboy outfit. I wondered whether he knew I was 'commando' again for only the second time in my hotel career.

"We were in bed, fast asleep when I felt the urge to move over having been told to do so by a strange voice, half asleep I did just that. It was only when my husband got up for the toilet that he noticed there were still two people occupying the bed he'd just left. He turned the light on and we found a naked man lying in our bed fast asleep."

I entered the room to find 'Steve' in the centre of someone else's bed curled up in their duvet snoring peacefully. "Now, what to do?"

I thought out loud, hoping for a suggestion. The audience was growing outside when I emerged to pacify the former occupants of room 10. I explained the story of the night before, unnecessary because the psychiatrist had already. I woke 'Steve's' partner and together we got him into her bed.

The lady from room 10 who had unwittingly had three in a bed but failed to appreciate her luck, admired 'Steve's' derriere on his short walk 'home'. The crowd dispersed and I got home to Sybil with a proper story that would definitely raise her eye patch of curiosity.

At breakfast the next day I struggled to make it in time for service. Just as I reached the restaurant door I saw 'Steve' addressing the room. He was apologising to them all and explained that he hadn't brought his medication that sometimes helped prevent nocturnal forays into the unknown. He made a special effort to appease the woman whose bed he'd shared and apologised if he had done anything inappropriate and for the shock. Blushing she replied "Having seen you walking back to your room afterwards, I only wish you had been inappropriate, I think we kicked you out too soon and I am so glad now that I forgot to lock the bedroom door last night!" To the roars of laughter from the other guests, the red face of one and to the relief of thine host.

But, as you all know, just when things are at their brightest and best, there's always a niggling worry at the back of your mind that someone is going to try and put one over on you. And in the case of an innkeeper, this nemesis could well be a hotel inspector.

"This is an elegant hotel!
Room service has an unlisted number."
Henny Youngman

6

Spoon Salesmen

But by the next year, things were going much better mainly because we now understood and managed our customers more confidently. Our "annus horribilis" was behind us as was my own personal one, now thankfully cured.

Business was very good, it was a hotel I could be proud of and now it was time to set our sights on a second rosette from the Automobile Association. We had reinvested all our profits and refurbished the seventeen ensuite bedrooms and common areas of the hotel; everything went, except the numbers on the bedroom doors. The hotel had long held a single rosette for fine cuisine but we hankered after a second, so, our latest expenditure was the complete replacement of every piece of equipment in the kitchens. We trashed all that was old and illegal and fitted it out with the sort of state-of-the-art 'as seen on Hells Kitchen' equipment.

Single rosettes may be dished out, based upon a snap inspection, but we were going for two, so were on our guard. It behoves every innkeeper to develop a nose for recognising those whose job it is to test establishments to the 'nth degree, taking the appropriate action.

The first person I contact once a 'suspect Spoon Salesman' has booked is Barbara Cannings, our 70-something Head Housekeeper, followed quickly by the head chef.

In 1975, Basil Fawlty mistook a spoon salesman (played by

Bernard Cribbins) for a hotel inspector, with hilarious consequences. Nowadays a guest being mistaken as a hotel inspector can
count himself more fortunate. He will be amazed at the quality of
service suddenly coming his way.

Many hotels of rosette standard, especially two and above, have
a list of inspector's names and their pseudonyms, checking any
'suspect bookings' against names on the list. It is better to know
than not to know, although they often make themselves bloody obvious, rather like police on a stakeout parking their white vans with
blacked-out windows for hours on end. Occasionally a door opens
and a sleep-deprived detective stumbles out with an empty poly-
styrene cup amidst a waft of cigarette smoke. 'Spoon salesmen' are
no different and often just as obvious.

The first telltale signs are the questions they ask when they
book, often appearing to read from a script. They normally book
as singles and don't often bother to give a reason for their visit.
They always request a table for dinner (businessmen rarely do this
because plans change) and they even book the dining time.

'Spoon salesmen' also request directions and ask about Internet
access, often only giving a mobile number as a way of contact. But
when they arrive, they always carry a laptop computer, order room
service and say 'yes' to a bedroom turn down (or as we now put it,
"Would you like your bedroom refreshed during dinner?"), which
involves emptying the bins, cleaning the toilet, turning back the
covers of the bed, putting on the bedside lamps, closing the curtains, putting a fold into the toilet roll, and placing a weather forecast and a chocolate on the pillow.

Add all that up and you know you've hooked a live one. If you've
got it wrong, some punter is going to get the service of their lives.

In the early days at Dial House, I cut my detective teeth on a few
'spoon salesmen,' but it wasn't as vital there, it being only an upmarket B&B with a "boil-in-the-bag" menu when I ran it. Now,
though, I can usually sniff out an inspector prior to arrival with

ease. All the staff on reception are trained to do the job the same way every time, which helps if we are challenged about the procedures. It also helps to make them aware of suspect punters, who will ask the usual unusual questions and always say 'yes' to an offer of any service.

A few years back, when all at the Elizabethan manor were first thinking about a second rosette, my attention was drawn to a booking from a Mr. Hodgson. His booking card was all I needed to see: single, directions faxed, table for one at 8pm, and estimated arrival at 3pm (time enough for a room service order). He was not, however, on our 'suspects list'. But my nose was twitching. Was he or wasn't he?

Maybe a new guy.

Barbara and her team set about spring-cleaning the bedroom and restaurant, and the chefs worked more tirelessly than usual. It's a bit silly really, since the bedrooms are always just as pristine, but I don't know any hoteliers who ignore the signs by doing nothing.

When Mr. Hodgson arrived I was around, but not at reception. The girl on duty did a fine job, but she was as sure that we had a 'spy' as I was. I waited around the corner, listening to every word, then I ran down to the village store to buy some slightly more upmarket chocolates for his pillow.

The afternoon and evening went fairly well, with all the staff preened to perfection and dancing like cats on a hot tin roof; the food was good and on time. Breakfast service seemed to go OK, although I was unable to get the two breakfast waitresses to utter a word to the man, instead choosing to hide behind the even dumber waiter, too petrified to speak.

After breakfast, inevitably inspectors go upstairs, returning minutes later to reception, where the bill is presented and paid. They leave to put luggage in the car and return brandishing a business card to identify themselves, but now they look more like the cat that got the cream. Then they ask to see me. I am always on hand just at the moment they unmask, ready to act in shock and horror that we'd been caught on the hop. It's a performance that I pride myself on and would, I'm sure, get an accolade from the Royal Academy of Dramatic Art if they'd bother to come and watch.

It seems that we had done OK and Mr. Hodgson increased our quality score by a single point, but he wasn't impressed enough with the food to award a second rosette. That was to come later. The mystery shoppers are normally guided as to what to order, so mostly they order similar things. This one was different. He chose all the items off the menu we'd least have wanted him to; true enough, it wasn't good enough to achieve the higher accolade.

During our debriefing, when he told me about his experiences as our guest, he asked me if we'd known he was an inspector. Of course, I answered with the usual confidence and smile befitting an experienced 'actor' and hotelier.

"No, you really caught us by surprise, Mr. Hodgson, we had no idea."

"Strange, that," he said, thoughtfully, "because when I went to the village store to buy some cough sweets, they asked me whether I was in Corfe on business or pleasure. When I said business and that I was staying at Mortons House, the shopkeeper said, "Really, they're expecting an inspector from the AA today – I have just had the owner in buying fancy chocolates for his pillow!"

I suppose I would have done better to have bought him some cough drops.

Once a young male guest seemed to take a shine to a distinguished gentleman inspector, asking me if I would make an introduction to him, or send a drink to his table.

I knew the older man was an inspector, because he'd been here before when he awarded us our coveted second AA rosette. I politely refused and said to the lad he was barking up the wrong tree. But I have often wondered whether these guys have a kind of radar system and whether he knew differently. As we now had two rosettes and were only dreaming of a third, I wondered whether an introduction might have 'enlightened' our inspector.

One inspection we actually requested occurred in 2004. The hotel had just completed building two rooms in a walled garden that conformed to the new Disability Discrimination Act. We used this Act to help us gain planning approval to alter our Grade II Star listed property from seventeen to nineteen ensuite bedrooms and later to twenty-one. The Tourist Board offered an inspection to see what rating we could achieve and advertise to those less able.

When Mr. McClintock arrived he was spotted early in his stay but, unusually, we changed none of the service for him, as we now offered as high a level as we could. True to our form, we were awarded a Gold award for service, rising from the Silver award the hotel acquired before our ownership. But the real test would be our efforts to impress with our new accessibility.

He went through the building with great attention to detail and a tape measure to match it. As the ground floor had been altered considerably to allow wheelchair access, I was confident we would pass. The two new bedrooms were specially designed, checked and built with every advice known to the industry about how best to accommodate the many variations of disability. However I hadn't thought to check that the builders had done as requested. The ramp leading from the car park was not the required 1:12 gradient; Mr. McClintock measured ours with a strange spirit level and confirmed it to be 1:8. When my uncle David had visited earlier that year, he had told me that this was the case when he entered the hotel in his wheelchair, complaining that it was an uphill struggle. I remember mentally dismissing his comment as rubbish, which only goes to show that you should listen to your uncle sometimes, his legs maybe less able but his mind is as sharp as the Global knives the chefs wield in the kitchen.

The whole ramp had to be dug up and rebuilt at the correct gradient. Despite all the attention to detail, we have learnt since how hard it is to accommodate every kind of disability; we simply do the best we can.

The best 'mystery shopper' we ever had around was in 2005, at this time we were on a merit list for a third AA rosette as standards had risen as had the expectations of guests, hotel owners and Spoon salesmen. 'Our' inspector booked a room for two people to share, saying that they were a couple visiting the area to house hunt. On check-in, however, just the "wife" showed up, full of apologies. She said that her husband couldn't make it and she would dine alone. She told reception that she expected to get some calls from local estate agents.

"Just put them through," she said.

At dinner, she read the property section of the local rag intently, engaging in little conversation with waiting staff. It was a clever ruse and fooled us completely. Inspectors may book a twin but never a double – so we had no idea we could have bought new spoons! I am so glad the GM kept his hands to himself, she was rather attractive!

In spite of all the fun and games, inspection is a perfectly valid way of assessing the performance of hotels and restaurants. But as we get wiser, so do the inspectors, and it's normally an enjoyable battle of wits. Sometimes you ring the alarm bells, and, fearing an inspector is in the house, you pull out all the stops and give a service second to none – only to find the guest to be Bernard Cribbins hawking cutlery in your Oak Room.

But our best weapon against the machinations of disguised inspectors is our Barb, which is why she is the first person I turn to when the alarm sounds.

In every business, especially the hotel industry, there needs to be one person like Barbara Cannings. Her title is Head Housekeeper, but she is so much more. Mortons House Hotel wouldn't be able to offer such a warm welcome without Barb. I have never worked with anybody like her. She is well over retirement age, but far more capable of a full day's work when those half her years cannot cope. She is five foot nothing and built to work. Irreplaceable.

Aged three score years and more than ten, she lives opposite the hotel in the house she was born in. Not the local mayoress, more like monarchy. Barb's mother worked here and with her she did her first housekeeping job aged eight, in the rectory. Always involved in the church, she was once in the choir and has been serving 'the blood of Christ' every Sunday for 30 plus years in her role as a lay pastoral helper. She is the treasurer of the Corfe Valley News, a monthly booklet delivered to every home in the Parish and on the committee for the local cemetery, God's Acre. When she wasn't housekeeping, she worked in most, if not all, of the local shops and she sang with a Big Band in the sixties.

When she is not at work, or working for us in 'her time', Barb is a volunteer Sunday school helper and walks her daughter's dog on the National Trust common. She and husband Johnnie dined here for the first time in 15 years in the year we took over. She now dines on her birthday every year, on us.

When we took over the hotel we were warned about Barb – but no one could really be like that, could they? She was reputed to be a great gossip, but although I have sometimes wondered exactly where rumours start in this small village, when I tried to get her to start one of my own – that the new owners were considering a change of use of the hotel to a brothel – it failed. So either she didn't believe me or she doesn't partake in local tittle-tattle. There is a great deal of gossip to listen to, if you are prepared to bend an ear. It didn't stop one young lady coming in for an interview for a job as a hostess. I didn't offer her a working trial though; Sybil was too close for comfort.

With someone like Barb to watch out for us an inspector's visit is often nothing to worry about.

It may upset and unnerve the staff, but it's lovely if you happen to be that wrongly identified guest. So, next time you book a room, do as the inspectors do and get the best service in town.

But you won't get good service unless the hotel has a star personality. And thankfully we have - and it is not me. But of course you guessed that already.

7

Perfectly Maid

I remember the excitement well. As soon as my brothers and I had been told we were visiting our grandparents in Woodstock, our spirits lifted. Not just because grandpa would fill our heads with stories of his World War II naval battles - Captain Money would hold court for hours, his three grandsons riveted, seated upon his knee - but because of the welcome and endless niceties put on by my grandmother. She knew each of her grandsons loves and prepared them in advance. I am not sure that I could put a finger on any one thing because everything was perfect, she made sure of that.

Not just the smell of the freshly laundered sheets on our beds, or the unsalted butter on her homemade bread, toasted and spread with her own marmalade, it was the feeling of being truly made to feel welcome and that she badly wanted us to be there.

I didn't know it then, but that was just the sort of welcome my hotel guests would get decades later, and I am sure many feel the same way I did, when they come back here, again and again.

Barbara Cannings reminds me of my granny. She makes the guests feel so at home in the hotel they normally leave on first name terms. Like granny she prepares in advance using our guest history, she recognises birthdays, anniversaries, and remembers faces and the strange quirks some have. And I, like Captain Money tell endless anecdotes to anyone interested, but never with them sat on my knee.

Barbara has her faults and the Head Housekeeper being blind as a bat maybe one. The others I have yet to find in more than seven years. Put simply she is heaven sent and God fearing. She does endless amounts for us in her own time ('Barb' time she calls it) and will stop at nothing to help a guest or her bosses out. She can do any shift in any department at anytime, except Sunday mornings when she is in Sunday school and church. She gives the welcome hoteliers dream about being able to offer and is by far the most written about member of staff, whatever the men in white coats or the maitre d'hotel think. She gets as many Christmas cards as Basil.

You probably haven't met her so I will have a stab at describing the other woman I love. She is a touch over 5 foot tall and built, well, to work. She is always the smartest of housekeepers and clearly full of pride (easily hurt, mind). She never stops talking, which is very useful when trying to delay guests while others prepare whatever is late, or hugely frustrating if you're waiting for her to take an order for something. Her local knowledge is second to none, although when she says "Dorset" we hear "Darrset." She rarely employs swear words and if she 'cusses' she may say "bugger" but that's about it. Oh, and we never cross on the staircase (neither did grandma) and she never stands still, rush, rush, busy, busy, rush, rush 24/7.

Intro done. Now recall for a moment what I have experienced in the hotel and tried to describe in this book. The only person who has seen it all before is Barb. Strange then that she seems to play the innocent, naïve and shock-horror part so well.

So it was important that we got off to a good start, but, early in our time at the hotel, I learnt a very important lesson. The customers may always be right, but they are often wrong, and shouldn't be trusted.

I was called in to appease guests staying in our Elizabethan Room, the honeymoon suite. They had complained bitterly after twenty minutes in the room that the sheets were dirty, and had gone out while the hotel 'dealt with it'. The simple thing for the staff to have done was to change the sheets and investigate later, but they called me and I called Barb at home after changing the sheets. I asked if she had forgotten anything at work today and told her of the complaint. She came across the thirty feet from her front door to the hotel at high speed and in an even higher rage. She was absolutely furious.

"What? Do you think I forgot to change the linen? No chance!"

Clearly, I'd have to engage all my charm to avoid tears, so I did, but even so she burst into tears and threatened never to set foot in the house again. The guests returned with me still in full charm mode (not mood), and they accepted my grovelling apologies along with a free bottle of bubbly. Later, I called the chambermaids who were on duty with Barb earlier; they all confirmed that the sheets had indeed been changed and could prove it with the laundry docket.

I'd upset Barb by questioning whether she'd done her job, had gone behind her back to ask the others she worked with the same question, and had given away a £50 bottle of splosh. The real answer was that the guests hadn't been truly honest about their first twenty minutes in the honeymooner's room. It would take time for her to trust me after this. It is not sensible to believe guests over some staff, I had discovered too late and to my cost.

She was to need my support a little time later and I was given a chance to redeem myself and win back some brownie points. A guest, part of a conference, who had been using our Castle Room, reported his mobile phone missing from his room after it had been 'refreshed' by the housekeeper.

At reception, he said, "My phone has been stolen from my room. It was there earlier and while I have been in the conference it has been stolen by one of your staff." As the company's business was important to us, I had to tread carefully, using all the possibilities to appease him: had he left it elsewhere? Was he sure it was in the room? As soon as the head housekeeper arrived at the scene she was accused of the theft. Barb was shocked and protested her innocence, I could see in her eyes she had not taken his mobile phone, she'd have had no idea how it worked anyway.

As is often the case when staff are confronted in this way, she was mortified and clearly close to tears again, her accuser was aggressive at his loss, finger pointing and nasty. I stopped short of the body search, or calling the police, as the guest had demanded. The hotel was searched and nothing found.

Out of the blue, Barb suggested we call the number of the missing phone to establish its whereabouts, which we did. It started ringing in a pocket of a heavy winter coat – which was held in the arms of her accuser. To his credit he later sent her a bunch of flowers with an apology in writing.

You wouldn't believe what guests leave behind in the rooms, or perhaps you would, but even I wouldn't had I not seen some of them myself. Whenever Barb finds something new, weird or wired, she will always bring it to the office to display, to watch the dismay or ask for guidance as to how it works and/or why?

One day, just as I sat toying with my Cappuccino at my desk I heard hoots of laughter coming from the honeymoon suite. A moment later Barb came into my office holding some long leather bondage straps. We all creased up when she said, "Boss, what on earth are these used for? The girls say it's something rude!" The explanation took only a minute or two before Barb's face blushed red like a beetroot and she burst into more hoots of laughter. Leather straps apart, there have been many occasions when she has come across items that were not meant to be seen by anyone, certainly not in the middle of a guest's stay.

One such occasion was the time the housekeepers took the opportunity to do a room while the guest was at breakfast. Returning from a good fry-up, the guest asked reception if the housekeepers could "leave the room today," but unfortunately it was too late, as

Barb was already at the office door telling Sybil and I all about her latest (or should I say latex) find. "It's a huge great big fat willy, made of black rubber and it must bloody hurt," she said. Just about then the guest reached the top of the stairs and there was an uncomfortable silence. The guests returned to the room and placed the 'Do Not Disturb' sign on the door, which remained there for the duration of their stay.

She regularly gets to see and hear enough to disturb most women of her age, but she takes it all in her stride. She can now tell the difference between a 'rampant rabbit' and a 'body massager.' She has had to log and store many such items in lost property. The strange thing is that no one ever asks for the return of anything so 'personal.' It hasn't stopped the mischievous streak in her, though; she is responsible for lost property and sending back to guests the items they have left behind. I am sure some 'things' go back with no disguise and without warning.

We often tease Barb about her end. When she's gone, we'll have her embalmed and put her on display in an open coffin and leave her at the top of the stairs. She won't need the space she has booked herself in God's Acre and this way she can continue to direct the hotel proceedings. The ghosts will miss her too. She has all the stories and tells them to anyone who'll listen. The one about the baby crying in the Elizabethan Room and children running up the stairs when the hotel is empty are her favourites.

She does so much more than her job. Rarely can she be heard complaining about her lot; sometimes, though, she does complain about the staff that I employ to 'help' her mainly because she can and does run rings around them. She returns to the hotel after her shift to deliver the mail to the Post Office and comes in on her days off to help with the laundry. She does this because she loves to; it also keeps her from being under Johnnie's feet at home.

Barb is also game for a laugh and won't give an inch because of age or stamina. So when we booked a company 'bonding day' to go

65

paintballing, she was keen and willing. Paintballing involves blasting the hell out of each other using air-powered guns. These fire bright yellow paint pellets that explode to indicate a direct hit, and they hurt.

Barb, being as blind as a bat, is hopeless at spotting cobwebs in bedrooms. But put her behind a scratched pair of steamed-up protective goggles and in a blue jumpsuit, looking like one of the Teletubbies, and she feels like an ace markswoman. She isn't the most agile of pensioners, but could outlast any young paintball warrior. She was a little out of position on a cold April morning in woodland around Poole, the terrain uneven and her sight so poor. I was her team captain and decided she would be best deployed protecting our flag. The other team, headed by Ted, would try to attack us and steal it. Simple. She sat behind a conifer barrier, 'her' flag behind her. I was behind her shouting instructions because I had to tell her where and what to shoot at, otherwise she'd 'kill' motionless trees.

All was going well. Every now and then she'd react to her commanding officer, pop up, and shoot anything that appeared to be moving. Barb and Basil were an unstoppable team and kept winning. But Ted's no fool, and he sussed the plan and mounted an attack, in numbers from two fronts. Barb was exposed as I defended an opposite flank. I shouted: "They're all around, Barb – fend for yourself!" Ted had eight people on her. As she stood to strut her stuff, they all opened fire at once. They covered her from head to foot in bright yellow explosions of paint. She'd been hit, and I had lost a good 'man' and subsequently our flag. I love Barb, but to see her recoil under the continued fire, being covered from head to toe in yellow paint, whooping and wailing, even squealing, was hard. I shouldn't have laughed, but it was unavoidable, that I laughed so loud and so long may have been. Barb is a great sport and took to being shot to bits rather well and laughed with me. Despite her 'death', the day was a bonding success.

I think Basil and Barb make a great team. She has made our time in Corfe Castle so much more enjoyable than anybody else and welcomed us like no other. She has never let us down, and often is responsible for keeping the show going. She never stops being brilliant.

I have joined her in so many laughs that I am happy to say that, if I had the choice to employ just one person to work with me, it would be Barb, no doubt whatsoever.

Achilles may have had a dodgy heel but if a hotel has a tender spot it must lie in the kitchen where one can experience the whole gamut of human emotions running rampant as the prima donnas of the skillet do their worst for the owner. I refer of course, to the men in white coats, the chefs.

Willard Marriott, asked for the most valuable advice he
could give to a traveller, replied:
"Always put the shower curtain inside the tub."

8

Men in White Coats

If the men in white coats arrive at the door looking menacing, you could be in for a lovely meal, or on the other hand perhaps a decent spell in a padded cell. The only thing missing from chef's whites are leather buckles at the end of each sleeve for tying the arms behind their backs when they finally flip and need sectioning under the Mental Health Act. That is if they don't get to you first, for they can and will drive you mental, literally.

"Service," I called, as loudly as a toastmaster announcing an important guest. I had three full English breakfasts to go and I had already called for a poached Kipper, topped with Milk foam to be taken away. I was doing another breakfast duty because a chef had let me down again. When nobody answered my call I bellowed again, only a little louder and now with a tinge of frustration. Then finally so loud that I'd bet the waiting staff holding the chefs up in the Swanage hotels, some four miles away, heard my scream.

A Manuel came to take away my efforts together with a burning glare from me that must have hurt his poor feelings.

Any good hotelier cannot live without them but it must be a hell of struggle living with a chef. Being married to one must be the ultimate fate worse than death.

I swear a lot of their attitude comes down to the fact that they refer to themselves as "chefs" and interpret this under its literal translation as "chief." For it means chief of the kitchen – and nowhere else, but try telling one that.

I mustn't mention the war but I can't help recalling that his minions often referred to Hitler as "der Chef," I suppose when he was cooking up plans to invade somewhere or other and I can often spot the similarities in my staff.

I know that it's hard to imagine the intense heat and pressure in a commercial kitchen unless you've been there. Needless to say it isn't like doing a Sunday roast at home. But as Harry Truman once remarked, "If you can't stand the heat, get out of the kitchen."

Unfortunately, they sometimes take his advice – at the most inconvenient times as far as the owner is concerned.

And in a hotel kitchen, everything you touch is hot, very bloody hot, the chef included. If it isn't hot it is surgically sharp. If it isn't hot and it ain't sharp then it shouldn't be in there. It's Hell's Kitchen, literally.

I could never do the job day in day out; I have neither the skill, the patience nor the body to cope. After only three days on the trot once, I got what is known in the snake pit as 'Chef's arse'. This is when the river of sweat runs down your spine and into the crack of your bum. Add in the simple fact that you are on the move all day and most of the evening it doesn't take much imagination to get to appreciate just how sore this can become, not helped one jot by the constant scratching that is so addictive, but this just makes it worse. So why scratch, I hear you ask? Put that question to any kid with eczema, they'll tell you it is ecstasy, until you stop and then the pain begins, as do the regrets. So next time when you spot the chef scratching, have a tinge of sympathy and hope he washes his hands afterwards.

Cooking in a commercial arena can be like a drug, it is addictive and sometimes as harmful. Some chefs make it to the top without dependence on alcohol or chemical stimulants but a good many don't. You either love it and live with the consequences, or love it and get out before it is too late.

Since taking over Mortons House I have seen four head chefs

70

come and go in seven years, but one only lasted a matter of months. I will say that I am on friendly terms with one of the departed arse scratchers, I remain occasionally acquainted with another and wouldn't speak to the other two. More and more rarely these days do chefs leave a job on good terms. The pressures are such that it normally takes little, at the wrong time, to bring down the relationship like a house of cards. You can be their mate and respected boss one minute and a complete c**t the next, and then off they walk, with their knives and some of your equipment, over the fence to where the grass is greener.

Just like restaurants with Michelin stars, the number of AA rosettes you have is all-important, to you, the customers, and the ego filled chefs. The more you have the higher the expectations of both customers and bosses. The loss of a rosette can be catastrophic to a business and the careers of both waiting staff and chefs. That's why it is often 'Hell in the Kitchen.'

When we took over Mortons House there was a new Head Chef – in fact, Dan arrived on the same day we did, not comforting news for us as new owners, I must say, especially as he had been employed after the exchange of contracts and before completion of the deal. The former owner should not have done this after the exchange of contracts without my permission and certainly not without my knowledge. But there was no point fretting over it – there were other things to worry about on the day we took over, like paying the Langford's for the privilege of doing so.

Dan was most memorable for his cooking ability, which was comfortably one rosette and for his likeable attitude. But this seemed to be accompanied by an inability to command the kitchen with any authority and a lack of organisation. During his time the costs and revenue figures were the worst we'd see in our time at the hotel. Chefs work to levels normally set by the owners. In a Pizzeria it is possible to achieve foods costs of 28% – I know, I did it. But in 'fine dining' establishments, the cost figures are closer to

71

35%, leaving the remaining 65% to pay the bills and the staff. Any balance is profit.

During the time Dan was the head chef, his costs averaged around 46%. It wasn't only his fault since we didn't know what we were doing then either. This was his first job as a head chef and my first outing in a fine dining establishment. This combination probably benefited both parties – he cut his teeth on us and we learnt from him what worked and what didn't at that level, the customers and owners were both very happy with what came out of his kitchen. Had we reduced the size of the menu from the ridiculous amount of options available then, we would both have found it easier to shine.

My favourite 'Dan' moment was our second Christmas. The endless supplies of mince pies required could put anybody off coming to work. So Dan employed his dainty fingered wife Sharon to help. Her pastry chef skills would be right up our street. Filo pastry and mincemeat at the ready Sharon was knocking out 140 delicate and beautiful, little festive treats, an hour. The regular chefs with the sore arses decided to try and match her. Five gave it a go but nobody got close, although Dan did manage 110. At first I thought chauvinistically that this kitchen was no place for a woman, but hadn't counted on Sharon fully justifying wearing the trousers as well as the white coat.

As many chefs do, Dan left us after a row. I had been woken to cook for one breakfast shift too many because a chef turned in late. I asked Dan why one of his team was so often late on duty for breakfast; and could he do something about it. His response, in front of his team, was something like: "Would you like me to call Wilts and Dorset Bus Company to ask them to run the buses on time?" I seem to recall replying: "No, you idle sarcastic twat, I just want you to organise your team properly enough to ensure we can serve breakfast at the advertised time!" I was clearly in chef speak mode. I later sought, and got, an equally public apology. Unfortunately the deed was done, all bar more shouting, because he handed in his resignation the next day.

I was grateful to see him and his wife Sharon last week, they popped in to show off their new daughter Felicity (Sharon's sixth). Time is a great healer, they say. I thoroughly enjoyed seeing them again so maybe 'they' are right.

Many an advert and word of mouth locally had failed to fill Dan's size twelve chef clogs. We had had a few applicants but most were of the deep-fat-fryer and micro-wave set from the local pubs. Very much *not* Mortons House.

We had a false start with one spineless fellow that we had chosen to take over from Dan, who never made it through the door to start work on his first day, nor did he bother to call. Panic stations ensued, as we had to protect our rosette status. So, with little time to start the interview process again, we allowed the Sous-chef to take over temporarily until we took on Craig.

Craig was one of the original applicants to replace Dan, but he had been overlooked because he was 'known' locally and had a colourful reputation, that's what I was told anyway. But despite this, he interviewed well and his draft menu looked more than good enough to eat. We offered Craig the chance to take us on to the next level despite some fears.

It wasn't long before our little Brummie-born chef had got the second rosette the team had worked so hard for and the owners craved. The menus and food standards had all improved sufficiently enough to move up one notch. The 'spoon salesmen' from the AA who inspected us in April 2004 was also very impressed by the new team in the restaurant, commenting that the service with the food was comfortably now worth two rosettes. We had underestimated Craig.

With this came more advertising and that brought 'Foodies' from afar to sample the new fare. The difference in the food quality, presentation and costs was as dramatic and instant as the customer response. This guy could really cook. I taste tested many ideas of his in my office before they hit the menu, his Oxtail tortellini being one of the finest, my favourite interruption and his best invention.

My culinary low point came while helping Craig out. I was charged with making the 'amuse bouche,' a complimentary appetiser served to our a la Carte guests before dinner. He wanted a Leek and Potato soup, easy, no problem, done it before at home, thought I. The thing is making enough for 45 is a little tougher. All went well until I seasoned the bubbling cauldron of my toil and trouble. Thinking that I should chuck in handfuls more than I do at home I cracked a fist full of black pepper into the pot. I had stirred it in before Craig appeared at my shoulder with a frown worse than my mother's. He'd seen my attempt at seasoning and now dipped his tasting spoon into the broth. It was billed as Black Pepper, Leek and Potato Soup on the menu that night as it is customary to put the lead ingredient first. Much of it came back from the dining room with only a teaspoonful missing.

As a remedy for blocked sinuses it would have been a roaring success I feel and I pointed this out to him, but he never stopped teasing me about my failure by suggesting it as an option whenever we wrote menus together.

When we lost our cleaver wielding Sous chef, Craig carried on, but he had reached and passed his peak in my employ. From then on our relationship ran like a roller coaster, going downhill from wonderfully happy and mutually beneficial, to mistrustful and then worse. He never actually let us down but the pressure got to him more than it did me. He was always there when others let him down and eventually that takes its toll.

When the end came it was far from sweet, so much so that if we see each other approaching in the distance it seems easier to cross the street than to pass by each other on the pavement. Sad as it is, this seems to be the way that these tense, pressurised and sometimes false friendships end. It is easier to remember the lows than the many, many highs.

He could really cook and got me out of many more holes than I could dig for him. He cost me a few bob though, he persuaded me to spend £120,000 on a new kitchen!

At Christmas 2006, a few years after he'd gone, I was reminded of his sense of humour, one that I had enjoyed plenty of during the good times. We had been 'mystery shopped' by Paddy Burt from the Telegraph newspaper. She is commonly very spiteful and sarcastic and rarely says anything complimentary even on the places she seems to like. Our review wasn't too bad but nasty enough to cause some customer comment later that month around the tinsel laden fireplace.

A few days later, when my anger at the hacks spiteful comments had yet to subside, I got a Christmas card. When I opened it, it was signed, Love Paddy Burt XXX. At first I thought about sending her a turd in a gift-wrapped box by return, to arrive in time for Christ's birthday. But on closer inspection Craig's handwriting was as easily recognisable as the Swanage postmark.

It had been a long time since he'd made me laugh like that, my mood lifted sufficiently to greet the fee-paying punters flooding in the door with a suitably festive smile.

The interview process for a new head chef started in earnest. One applicant stood out, head and shoulders above the rest. They say that you can't kid a kidder, but I was hooked on the yip yap and rabbit I had from the applicant in front of me. A four-hour first interview with me is unheard of, until now. He talked the talk and I offered him the chance to walk the walk on a very decent salary.

As a gesture of goodwill I purchased two pieces of kitchen machinery that my new number one had casually mentioned during our marathon interview. Some gesture, having shipped a good load of cash on the new kitchen a few months before. These he said, "Were not essential, but would be nice to have." Before he started, the hotel was five grand lighter after the purchase of a vacuum packaging machine, and a Pacojet. One saved us money and wastage, the other made amazing ice-creams and sorbets to order in minutes.

The honeymoon period never got going. The head of department departed after a few months leaving mostly bitter memories and broken teams behind him. His mood swings may have been chemically induced but his departure came not a minute too soon to the applause of all who remained.

Kid a kidder? He got me hook, line and sinker.

In through the front door came a Knight in shining armour. I had released the 'temporary' head chef from his contractual duties early in order to spare the staff and customers from more of his pain in the arse. For the first time in my career, I entrusted our rosettes, customer satisfaction and personal sanity to a highly paid mercenary with a decent record. Derek arrived at the reception desk just as 'all mouth and no trousers' left through the tradesman's exit after service. I lined up twelve shot glasses and filled them full of Sambuca before calling in all the staff. Calling a toast to the end of our hell we raised a glass to our Knight from Anfield.

What followed was a period of constant improvement in standards that got us within a whisker of a third rosette. Derek brought in his trusted number two, Dave, a big fella, bigger personality and great help. Also called in was our current number one, Ed. Ed took over from Derek when it all went wrong.

Derek introduced me to Ed when I was 'picking' a dozen Frissee lettuces wearing my 'straight jacket' and chef pants. This involves taking out the whitest and undamaged leaves and discarding the greener more bitter parts. As kitchen wastage was the bane of my tenure at Mortons House, I saved more than I should have. So when Ed offered to take over from me, I was happy to leave for the peace of my office despite Sybil being there. But before the swing door closed behind me three quarters of my handiwork went in the trash. Derek may have waited a little longer but the result would've been the same, high standards these boys, I remember thinking.

We, the owners worked more closely with this team than any before it. I was as close to the operation as I dare be. Indeed Derek always said it was his personal highlight of his time here when I worked for him in the kitchen when he was in trouble in his first three weeks. Now I don't profess to be in his league but he very much appreciated the owner's commitment to ensure the highest standards were met by being there when he needed me. He taught me loads and showed me the way, his way and it worked out.

I shared a love of football with my team and we followed each game involving our teams as carefully as the service of his creations to the guests. He often helped me with my home cooking and this advice was invaluable when trying something new in my kitchen.

My personal high point was pulling in some favours from some very old contacts. After he had watched his beloved Liverpool in Istanbul win the Champions League final, we presented Derek with a signed squad picture of the moment when Dudek saved Shevchenko's last penalty. He was gob smacked for the first time.

The low points were few and far between; maybe his choice of girlfriend was one. She was the restaurant manageress until he stepped in, which caused untold strife within a settled team. It wasn't a great shock though; we'd seen a twinkle in his eye for a while before he moved in on the defenceless little doe. When that relationship ended it cost us three of the original cast. You can take the Scouser out of Liverpool but not Liverpool out of the Scouser.

That our professional relationship ended was the biggest downer. A minor row with a waiter turned into a major skirmish. Derek was holding a soup ladle and the less important plate carrier decided to wrest it from his grasp. If only the head chef hadn't resisted, the unfinished edge of the utensil might not have ripped out the tendons in the third finger of his chopping hand.

What had been so good and promised so much more came to an abrupt end after plastic surgery to repair the damage. Rather than take the piss and go sick for a year, Derek did the decent thing and left as soon as he was able to shake hands, free of pain. He stepped aside for Ed to take over.

We often babysit Derek's daughter Emily Beth and meet up to talk football or eat in the Castle Inn, just up the road, for lunch on a Sunday. He pops in for the best coffee in Dorset and we can reminisce with a smile.

At the time of writing Ed still heads the kitchen and we are still talking.

The acid test for any kitchen comes with the taking of multiple bookings by the owners, unaware that they should have consulted with the staff first, and weddings, in particular, provide a challenge of some magnitude.

9

Four Weddings and a Funeral

Marriage is an institution greatly favoured by divorce lawyers but, in spite of this dubious recommendation, it remains surprisingly popular.

Almost as soon as we got our feet under the desks of the Elizabethan manor, we applied for a licence to hold civil wedding ceremonies. After all, there we were in the most romantic setting imaginable complete with a bridal suite, so it seemed a natural thing to offer those about to get hitched at least a few moments of happiness before it all went downhill.

The previous owners had considered this a bad move because it was a huge amount of work for little increase in financial reward to hold ceremonies at the hotel. They felt that, because the hotel was almost always full at weekends, they had no need to replace the core business that the hotel was renowned for with the much harder wedding trade. The extra effort and staffing of weddings, they thought, meant the extra income wasn't enough to justify doing them at all.

But we were young, enthusiastic and more romantically inclined, so to us it made sense. Into the wedding business we plunged.

Brides seem to start planning their wedding day before they reach puberty. It's the fault of all those magazines for women, of course, which have nothing better to do than to put foolish ideas into the heads of susceptible pubescent youngsters wearing rose tinted specs. And, since they explain how to plan a perfect wedding, if anything goes badly wrong on the day, it never seems to be the bride's error, however much she has been involved in the schedule and execution. After all, the magazine told her how it should be done.

By the time the great day arrives, nerves are at breaking point and even the slightest hiccup can send the whole proceedings into chaos. And who will get the blame if the ceremony is to take place at an inn? Right first time. Thine host, Mr Fawlty.

Staffing the ceremony and wedding breakfast that follows is always a trial, some employees are expected to work obscene hours to ensure continuity and to try and achieve the levels of service the bride has been dreaming about for decades, having read about it in her magazines. When it goes well, it often goes very well; when it goes badly, it can be hell.

Add the influence of alcohol to festering family feuds, an unfortunate choice of words during the speeches, or the most trivial incident like the groom getting caught in the cloakroom with his trousers around his ankles and the maid of honours legs wrapped around his waist just a moment before the ceremony. Any number of folk are ready to blow their top; add to that one tired Basil and an overworked team, and the 'fun' and games begin.

Sometimes it can be both happy and a sad day for all, when nothing goes wrong.

Mr Greenish and his partner had stayed with us regularly during our first year in Corfe Castle. The couple were popular with the staff, with whom they always made an effort, and they shared life experiences with the new owners.

Soon after we had displayed our civil wedding licence in the reception area around November 2001, Mr Greenish enquired about holding his wedding here. As he was one of the first to benefit from our new status, there were plenty of dates available and he seemed eager to arrange the ceremony quickly. I was shocked when he explained to me why this was; his long-term partner had a brain disease that was an incurable terminal illness. I was never aware that there was anything unusual or wrong with his partner until their latest visit. Mr Greenish explained that he did not have very long to arrange the ceremony.

The staff had noticed the deterioration in the bride's condition in the weeks prior to the wedding day during their visits to make the necessary arrangements for the big day. Every effort is always made to ensure that couples getting married here have their needs met, but somehow we all tried a little harder – maybe because it was one of the first ceremonies, or maybe we cared more because of the situation? The planning was immaculate; every detail was checked and double-checked. The registrar from Weymouth was fully versed and prepared.

The evening before the ceremony I had to get over the shock of seeing the bride-to-be in a wheelchair. She had been an articulate, amusing and very friendly customer since we first met. It was very hard to see her now, barely able to hold her head up and to recognise me. The groom told me he hoped she would walk the aisle; I doubted but hoped hard with him.

On their big day, the weather was brighter than the bride's prospects. The registrar had arrived at the hotel early enough to interview both bride and groom, separately, as is her duty. Having spoken to Mr. Greenish and satisfied he was both of sound mind and happy to continue, she met with the bride. When she came out of the room, she was close to tears. The registrar explained that as she knew the situation she would overlook the fact that it was impossible to get the answers she needed from the bride. So Ted and I carried the wheelchair bound bride down the main staircase for the main event.

The ceremony took place not a moment to soon; indeed, it was almost impossible, due to the dramatic deterioration in the bride's health. Once over, there was applause and cheering from the invited guests; this only just masked the many tears being shed. Everyone wished it had been a month earlier, including me.

I have always been accused of being over-sensitive, along with a good many other less desirable traits, and this time I found it easier to cry a little than to be Basil.

We never saw them celebrate an anniversary or heard from them again so feared the worst and that the inevitable had happened.

Till death us do part was about right, I thought.

Back in the summer of 2003, there was a heat wave that lasted about ten days from late July into August, with temperatures constantly on or around 30°C (86°F). As I explained, this was entirely my fault, however at least somebody was thankful for a dose of global warming, the 'Grockles' arriving in their droves loved it, but then, they were the ones making us work in the heat.

Sybling and Ted were away on holiday, so I was about to do fourteen days on the trot. It was without doubt the hardest period I have ever experienced on the job as the hotel was more than 90% full over the summer months.

We were fully staffed one minute; the next we weren't. Four key staff disappeared just before the first of three weddings that we had taken bookings for. First, I had dismissed my Sous-chef for gross misconduct; he had threatened a member of the waiting staff with a twelve-inch meat cleaver over some personal grievance and I didn't want one of my waiters to become the cut of the week. His partner was the restaurant manageress and, with that fidelity of lovers so often mentioned in song but seldom ever in real life, she had left with him, without notice.

This was not a good time for my assistant restaurant manager and his waitress partner to take compassionate leave to visit his dying father in Portugal, but what could I say?

Without my partners, I was down to the bare bones, which in

this case happened to be mostly Sybil and me. Furthermore, this was during Colin's latest sabbatical to determine if the grass grew greener elsewhere, so he too was absent. The hotel looked strikingly like the Marie Celeste, under full sail but with no crew.

And so on Thursday 7th August 2003, I awoke on the day of the wedding of Debbie Morrice to Jake Rakiura feeling tired and drained – and the day hadn't even begun. My departed GM and Sybling had done all the planning, but with neither present it meant that I had to read their notes very thoroughly and I had done three dress rehearsals already, none of which seemed to have gone right.

Jake and Debbie wanted the perfect day, as every couple does, but for Debbie the reasons were different. Their original plan was to marry on Stewart Island, or Rakiura Island (Jake's family name) as the Maoris call it. It's off the coast of New Zealand, and its name means "The Land of the Glowing Skies." It sounds an idyllic spot but because of her father being ill, they changed their plans to the rather more adjacent location of Corfe Castle and Mortons House Hotel. Sadly this change of plan and venue had come too late for her father, who passed away before he got to lead Debbie down the aisle.

I had already upset the bride-to-be before the wedding. The hotel had been trying to contact her for two weeks with no response, and I'd sent a letter asking her to call to finalise arrangements. Receiving no response, in panic I let the Basil side of me slip out a bit and sent a compliment slip with another, shorter note, stating that we couldn't guarantee their special day if we couldn't talk through final plans and numbers. Now if that didn't get a reaction nothing would.

None of Colin's notes had mentioned her bereavement, so I walked right into her anger and grief when she finally made contact and came in to see me. Unfortunately, Colin had also failed to note that she and Jake were away on holiday before the wedding, as much to recover from her loss as to prepare for the big day without her father, hence the lack of response. It took me a good couple of hours to reassure her that I understood all the arrangements and details of her previous meetings with Colin and that I had control.

She told me later that the hotel where Jake had proposed to her was now owned by a Basil Fawlty character, and she had feared her big day was being run by another not dissimilar chap – namely me.

The first problem that greeted me on arrival at the hotel was a couple of large and very expensive Koi carp floating upside down in the pond and another two swimming around in circles on their sides, like bad synchronised swimmers but without the fixed grin. The bigger fish were worth about £500 each but thankfully, 'Goldie' the ghost carp, the one my children favour was not one of them. I rang our 'fish man' and Koi expert, Richard. He asked me a few fishy questions and said he'd come on Saturday, to check things out. He recommended that I cleaned the filters.

The job of cleaning the pond's filters while Ted is away falls to me. These got filthy much more quickly in the heat than he had warned me. The pond was popular and drew a daily audience from the lunchtime diners on the terrace and those enjoying the early evening sunshine. The pond filters had to be kept clean, but I hated the job of cleaning endless buckets of fish shit from them. I had already cleaned them four times in the first week Ted was away so I was confident the dead fish weren't anything other than a coincidence and not my doing. Fish, other than cooked, are not my thing.

Having finished by the pond, the next problem was that the round tables ordered specially by the bride had not turned up. The company said they were "on their way," which was much like saying that the cheque was in the mail as far as I was concerned. It was late and we didn't need this added trauma. It takes hours to lay a wedding table properly, and our restaurant manager, having followed her heart a few days earlier along with the sous-chef, was no longer with us. The new staff were not capable of laying the tables alone, so it was left to me to organise. The heat was almost unbearable and the entire staff, those still employed and left standing, were dressed in their best outfits for the occasion. We would have been better in shorts and bare chests in the heat.

Debbie and Jake's wedding was to be an afternoon ceremony followed by champagne and canapés by the pond with the wedding breakfast (why do they call it a breakfast?) due to start at 6 o'clock.

We had offered exclusive use to the wedding guests, which in this case meant the use of all bedrooms and our taking no non-resident business.

One job for me that morning was to stock the bar. In doing so, I passed the pond and saw that the two not-so synchronised swimmers were nearly dead and floating on their sides. Richard got another call.

"Are they gulping at the surface?" he asked. They weren't really, no more so than usual, I thought, fish always gulp, don't they? This diagnosis seemed to satisfy him so he said he'd be happy to come two days later to check them, but I already had lost over £2000 of fish in two days and none that I could cook.

As I carried the empty bottles around the pond to the storage area, the stench at the back of the hotel was overpowering. The fat trap, the thing that catches ALL of the kitchen waste, was full and had set solid. It had started overflowing producing a shockingly sickly-smelling honk, one breath of which had me retching. It was great to see Barb and a new waiter mopping up the 'sludge from hell,' but unfortunate that neither had thought to shut the restaurant windows or those to the guest bedrooms just above. The whole restaurant and these four rooms were by now indescribably odoriferous.

Having washed my face and hands I was now a little paler than I'd like and was called to the kitchen, where the few chefs we had left had a mammoth catering job to do in the rising temperatures. I was told there was a chance we wouldn't be ready, as Craig (the then head chef) didn't have enough hands to cope, and those around him were paid temporary mercenaries recruited from the village or our young and inexperienced trainee chefs who seemed to be going around in circles like the dying fish. The kitchen was 47°C (117°F) – an illegally high temperature to work in, although no one knew this but me. I wasn't telling either and quietly confiscated the thermometer. The Pimms sorbet wouldn't set: the ice cream maker just couldn't cope, so a chef was dispatched to whisk it in a freezer – a job for which everyone volunteered even though he came out a delicate shade of blue himself.

The oak-panelled drawing room was made ready for the ceremony due to start at 4:00 p.m. – time enough for two more fish to float to the surface in the pond and the round tables to arrive.

Debbie had arranged for a piper to 'bring in the spirit' of her late father as the guests entered the room for the wedding. Clearly emotions were running high, as was my blood pressure. We had just twenty minutes to prepare the strawberries dipped in white and dark chocolate that were to be served with the Kir Royales to all the guests after the ceremony. Staff from all areas started dipping fruit into melted chocolate and then putting them in the freezer to set; they then poured 50-odd glasses of champagne to be topped with crème de cassis. Job done we rushed back to lay the tables that had just arrived and were now in situ. The head chef told me he'd be ready for 6:30pm – but the function was booked for 6:00pm

The guests paraded around the pond after the ceremony, sipping their blackcurrant-flavoured champagne, commenting on our floating dead fish and questioning whether carp was on the menu that night, ha bloody ha.

At least Debbie and Jake had perfect weather for the photo-taking session around the lovely Elizabethan building. Meanwhile the clock for the chefs kept ticking.

No matter how many clock-watching visitations I made to the

kitchen, the predictions were the same, as was the temperature.

It was about time to take the party into the dining room, but alarm bells were ringing somewhere in my head – also, it turned out, in the hotel as well. A quick scan of the new fire alarm control panel suggested that somewhere in the new wing we had a smoke detector alert. A rather observant new waiter came running towards me shouting Fire! Fire! If only he'd been called Manuel I could've poked him in the eye but we were short of staff. There's an old saying that there's no smoke without fire and an incendiary wedding seemed on the cards.

A full hotel evacuation looked like the only option, something that was going to go down like a lead balloon with a hotel full of hungry people waiting for the banquet.

I soon found the alert came from a sensor outside Room 14 and was simply a false alarm. I cleaned it and reset the alarm. Two minutes later, the same sensor set the alarms off again. I went through the clean-and-reset procedure again; again the alarm bells rang out. I muttered a few four-letter superlatives a little louder than I should of as I was on my way back to reception, I was overheard by a woman wearing a ridiculous hat whose tuts were as loud as my rantings.

Since it was pointless to bring in the guests for a wedding breakfast with this racket in competition with the piper, although personally I thought it was more tuneful, I had the staff stall them by pouring more champagne, but this time on Basil.

A call to our alarm people, who service the system, was made. The engineer, who I suspect was not trying to organise a wedding reception at the time, was calm and reassuring. He explained it was probably merely a fault with the sensor, which could be by-passed. All I had to do was to get the maintenance man to wire that location in series, but in the absence of Ted, I was the maintenance man – and I hate electrics. I can electrocute myself re-wiring a plug! But I had no time to protest. He told me what to do, but at 5:55pm I only had five minutes before the guests would be seated for the wedding breakfast.

There was no time for ladders, but I could just reach the wires behind the sensor; all I had to do was connect red-to-red and black-to-black he had said, cheerfully. It was a simple job, or so he told me, but it was made harder by the stifling heat upstairs. I was suitably apprehensive that at any moment 240 volts might course through my veins, but I got the job done without any more unwanted shocks to my system and mercifully silenced the bells.

I rang the alarm company, and the engineer confirmed that the system was now safe; indeed, I had been too all along, since he explained that as there were only 12 volts running the sensors, I needn't have sweated and stressed so much. Had he mentioned that earlier, I wouldn't now have had the kind of psychotic glazed pallid expression I was wearing.

I changed my sweat soaked shirt and tie and ushered in the guests, leaving Jake and Debbie until last.

"Please be upstanding for the bride and groom," I bellowed in my best toastmaster voice, as if all was well.

The happy couple walked in and gave me a smile. By the time we unfolded the napkins, served bread and poured the wine and water, the first course arrived from the kitchen. Craig and his diminished team had got up to speed during the timely delay while I, in the unlikely guise of the maintenance man, had silenced the fire alarms. Even the Pimms sorbet came out perfectly set. The guests were clearly loving it, but my frequent visits to the kitchen showed me how little the chefs were.

Craig's eyes were glazing over showing he was clearly done for; he had done a fabulous job achieving the quality demanded and in the time available, given the staff shortages and the heat.

I sent him home to rest but he left for the pub after the final course was delivered to the wedding guests. I wondered if he'd ever come back.

The staff had a sweepstake on the total length of time the speeches would last. There are normally three: the groom, then the bride's father, followed by the best man. Each member of staff who wanted to enter put in a guess and a fiver. I guessed 38 minutes, but 22 won it – I had forgotten that there was no bride's father to speak. I could get nothing to go my way that day.

After the speeches and toasts, the bride and groom cut the cake, to more picture taking. Then the guests started to drift out and relax around the ground floor. There was a lot of clearing up in the restaurant, but at least it only needed laying for the wedding party's breakfast the next day. The rest of the work was needed in the bar.

I had enough staff on duty to handle this and contemplated a short walk home. Instead, I decided to wind down by having a glass of wine and my single daily cigarette on the terrace, which had finally begun to cool off.

It was now that I began to consider seriously that our predecessors, the Langfords, might have been right about not wanting to do weddings.

Just as I had taken my first gulp of my chosen Merlot and drawn long and hard on my nicotine stick, I noticed more Olympic hopefuls swimming in circles and another large carp floating lifelessly on the surface. Why were they dying and what could I do? I sat with my head in my hands very close to exhaustion, despair and tears, thinking enough already!

I didn't notice Debbie or Jake approach, but in my misery I heard what they said. They thanked me for a perfect day, thanked me for all my effort and asked me to praise the chefs and all the staff. Then Debbie said something that finally reduced me to tears.

"Well done, what a show you and your team have put on. I never doubted you for one minute!" she joked, "Thanks ever so much you must be chuffed that it all went to plan, Andy."

When Jake quipped "money for old rope I'd say." I was barely able to raise a wry smile before running through the challenges the day had presented me. The newlyweds had no idea at any stage that the hotel had so nearly let them down so badly so many times. "The best actors in the world must be in the hotel trade," said the newly wedded Debbie and then, "You deserve an Oscar."

By the time our pond expert arrived on Saturday morning, we had lost eleven fish. Eight were of a good size and the lot was worth around £5000. I was sad, but I hadn't seen the problem gawping at me from the pond; they weren't hungry – they were suffocating. In the continual heat, the plants in the water produce carbon dioxide, not oxygen, if only I had listened in Biology lessons. To prove his point, the expert asked me to spray the water, using a hosepipe, thus creating a flume of bubbles. The fish danced in this lifeline, clearly loving every second. It was the last time we'd have a problem like this, as Richard fitted air stones and a pump along the whole length of our pond, and these produced more than enough oxygen in any weather. Thankfully, Goldie was safe -the biggest carp and obviously one of the toughest, as many of the largest perished first.

But not all the weddings were quite as uneventful or as peaceful!

Two local Coppers had booked their wedding ceremony in a registry office, followed by a dinner celebration and a karaoke evening at the hotel. The event took place just before Christmas. Due to the size of the party, and their desire to have a karaoke machine, which I personally consider to be the Japanese way of getting their own back, we insisted the bride and groom booked every bedroom and the entire hotel for the duration of the weekend.

The hotel was exclusively 'theirs' from Saturday morning until check-out time on Sunday. It would have been impossible to offer any unused rooms to non-wedding guests as they would not have been able to dine, and unless they joined the party, which spilled into all ground floor rooms, there would be no escaping the karaoke. The period leading up to this busy weekend was marred by late cancellations by some of their invited guests. The rooms left unused would be charged to the bride and groom's account (as had been explained and agreed). The bride now seemed unwilling to accept that it was she who had insisted on booking all the rooms and had agreed to their exclusive use on the basis that they paid for all the rooms. Jenny, the bride, now wanted us to try and sell rooms to any takers in order to reduce her bill; it seemed unlikely that we would be successful, but we agreed to try and see if we could come up with a few Karaoke lovers. The period before Christmas is a popular time and, as with most weekends, we anticipate being full. Unfortunately, as the date approached we had few takers for a weekend away without dinner but with free karaoke! So three bedrooms remained empty when the big day arrived. Sybling was asked to address any details about cancellation charges and any explanations directly to the groom, Adrian. Jenny, she was told, "had lost confidence in her." An uneasy agreement was reached rather like Munich in 1938.

All the 'troubles' seemed forgotten on the day, as everybody was intent on having a ball. I had the dubious honour of working that day; sometimes the rota was cruel, I thought, as it would have been better for it to be the organiser's day on duty but Sybling had other plans. I would have to be on my best behaviour and give the full works to ensure a faultless service, given the bride's misgivings. When called upon to be attentive, thoughtful and observant, I still believe I can do it as well as anyone, despite my Basil tendencies and all too quick (these days) sarcastic wit.

I have to say that I thoroughly enjoyed making the extra effort; guests were also reacting well to the 'service with a smile attitude' with an added anecdote thrown in for good measure. I do love entertaining and seem able to spot the best and most enthrallable guests from a mile off. This party was no exception, and I was able to attend to all the invited guests, who by now were separated by their preferences of after-dinner entertainment. The young men were in the bar, drinking like fish and almost as synchronised; the elderly relatives were by the fire in the Oak Room; those who knew they couldn't sing were in the Castle Room with the karaoke; this left the girls who didn't want to sing or drink to gossip in a bar lounge. I had to play my tune differently in each room like a Jukebox, tailoring my jokes and anecdotes according to taste. But this left two guests without a friend in the party, indeed, no one to play with – Shane and Kit, the only two children invited.

I showed them all my card tricks and told them all my child-friendly jokes whilst manning the reception desk; the switchboard was conveniently silent. Their mother told me that she was grateful of the break when she returned from seeing their father, who was a hit in the karaoke room. Shane was having a moment of reflection as he sat by the guest phone in front of my huge reception desk. He was bored and I was feeling a bit mischievous; so I stood and picked up my reception phone and dialled 229 and the antique guest phone rang next to him. Shane hesitated for a minute, only lifting the strange-looking receiver to his ear after his mum egged him on. She had seen my wink and sensed the need to play along. Holding the "talky bit" up to his mouth, Shane said "Hello?" in a quiet little voice. I asked him for his name and got an answer; I told him that I was Santa Claus and asked him for any ideas he had for Christmas presents he wanted. I got a lengthy list. Hiding the phone behind my jacket gave few people any clue to the ruse. Shane had no idea it was the host. His mother seemed as shocked as her boy, but my face remained straight. I ended by telling my young stooge that if he was a good little boy, there was a chance – just a chance – that he'd be lucky, but he mustn't peek if he saw me carrying my sack to fill his stocking, though. He put the 'old' receiver down and jumped up and down in delight, turning to his mum and shouting: "Mummy, I have just spoken to Santa!"

Mum then fetched Kit, and the process was repeated, with similar success and results; the old folk in the Oak Room were riveted and thought it was a hoot. I called from there because this time I thought the older brother might have sussed me out if he'd seen me hide my face and phone in my jacket at reception. The boys had been recharged and as their second wind started I said my goodbyes and wished their dreams true.

When I left the hotel late that night, I took great care to say goodbye to all the guests, especially the bride. Jenny had asked me to pose with her for a picture with Adrian, her new husband. She thanked me, as many others had, for a wonderful day and my special attention. As I walked to my car I was sure that everyone would remember this day for the right reasons. I had worked harder than I had for years but had enjoyed every minute. The staff we had on duty that day worked no less hard but were less obvious in their attempts to ensure the success of the biggest day in Jenny's life than I was.

So it came as a big surprise at the reception desk the following morning when Sybling was asked by Jenny to discuss her bill in her room. Although Sybling was thankful this was not at reception, she had not counted on a committee awaiting her arrival in the honeymoon suite. Trained police negotiators set about using their skills to intimidate and upset my poor sister-in-law. The groom went to the bathroom to avoid the confrontation, as he didn't agree with any of her complaints. Sybling returned to the room with a new bill, having removed one of the cancellation charges under duress; she had also been asked to remove the discretionary service charge.

"Was the service not worthy of our charge?" Sybling asked her. The bride responded that the service was as fabulous as the food, and that everyone had been very impressed, but, as it was a discretionary charge, the bride wanted to exercise her discretion and have it removed.

The bride gained from this a 10% reduction in her bill. Despite having a clear agreement about unused rooms (fully understood by the groom), it was this that caused her to make a point; as neither the limited company that owns the hotel, nor any of us, the directors, benefit in any way from guest gratuities, it was a wasted point. But the staff who worked so hard to make this the best wedding function the hotel has ever hosted and to gain the positive comments of all the departing guests (except one) would be the only ones to suffer – and suffer greatly they did.

The bride walked from the hotel without a single word of well deserved thanks, whilst Adrian called Sybling later that day and again the day after to apologise for Jenny's behaviour. He also promised to send a cheque to cover the staff gratuity. We are still waiting, as the cheque never arrived. When I told the staff they had got no thanks, one quipped "Don't worry we can't drink a thank you in the pub anyway!" I didn't have the heart to tell him the truth.

But the one I really felt sorry for was the groom. We only had to put up with her for a few hours; his might be a life sentence.

The reason the hotel describes the service charge as discretionary is because it is exactly that. Leaving it entirely up to guests with no suggestion often leads to it being 'overlooked'. However, if we included a service charge that was not discretionary, staff would then see a reduction of 17.5% from every tip, because it would attract Value Added Tax. The net amount they received would drop considerably, as Income Tax and National Insurance is already deducted. Our system works most of the time and is only an issue occasionally, as we only indicate a tip on weddings and large celebrations. But when the system goes wrong it can go horribly wrong.

The wedding of Tim and Sara was unremarkable in size and the challenge this celebration of marriage posed to us. It only became amazing at the end.

The parents and in-laws had been paying off chunks of the anticipated bill during a period of about a year before the big day; so, by the time the guests started arriving, there was likely to be little outstanding to bother the groom.

The menu was chosen, and the majority of the 40 guests were starting with a pressed terrine of duck and Griottine cherries served with Madeira syrup, followed by slow-roasted leg of Dorset lamb with marinated new potatoes and crushed root vegetables. The dessert was a summer pudding with seasonal berries and cream.

The ceremony went perfectly, the weather was fine, and everyone enjoyed the canapés and Pimms served on the terrace. They came into the restaurant on time and the food was served to everyone's delight and satisfaction. The speeches went off without any problems and I even won the staff 'speech sweep' with a bet of 31 minutes.

There were no overnight guests with this wedding; Tim and Sara were off on honeymoon after the cake cutting. We expected the other guests to leave by 5:30pm, after which we could concentrate on our weekend dinner - B&B customers, 46 of them in all on this Saturday in May.

Nobody was prepared for what was to come. Everyone had had a great time, no complaints just gushing praise, once again I was the proud barman, maitre d'hotel and squire all rolled into one. The guests gathered in reception to see off the bride and groom, who had just been presented with their bill for the outstanding balance; essentially this was no more than drinks on the day and the service charge.

I quickly realised that Tim and his mother were talking in whispers about the bill. I approached and asked if all was well and if there was a problem? Obviously there was an issue; Tim was looking flustered, even red. He already looked very much like Phil Mitchell had in Eastenders, I thought, and his brother, the best man, could easily have been Grant. Mum commented that they were not expecting a service charge; I replied that this was confirmed in the original meeting and subsequent contract that had been signed by both the hotel and the 'happy couple'. I produced the same and pointed out to them that we add a discretionary 10% to the total bill for service. Being like Phil and Grant Mitchell, the brothers, now grim, probably didn't know what 'discretionary' meant; they could simply have asked for it to be removed from the bill. As the service they'd gotten was near perfect, I didn't offer this information.

The contract was clear, they had a copy and appeared ready to pay without further comment, but they clearly hadn't budgeted to have a £400 increase to their bill.

At this point, the groom produced a chequebook. Our contract also states clearly that we only take bank drafts, cash or have cleared funds on the day. Personal cheques can only be used if the cheque guarantee card covered the total amount and I'd yet to see one to the tune of £900! I asked him if I could pass the card through our machine, thus gaining a guaranteed payment. With 39 others around him, he agreed. This was becoming a scene, so, moving my receptionist to one side, I processed the transaction myself. But like David Banner trying to hide the Hulk, I could feel Basil emerging.

The transaction went through with no problems after Tim entered his PIN. I waited for the receipt, which never came. When I checked, I found that our machine was out of paper! This was not good: he had no copy and worse, I had no confirmation. Quickly I dispatched a member of staff to the hotel office to get another roll. I used this time to make polite conversation with the bridegroom who, with his party, was becoming more than a little restless. I was just about to ask another stupid question about his day, trying to fill the time, when he said: "Listen, mate, if you are about to ask me for any more money, then I'm going to fucking head butt you!" I was shocked, but I could see the blood vessels on his shaven head bulging, as were those of his brother and best man.

"Would Sir like a stool to stand on to try that?" – Basil was out and on display. I was at least a foot taller than the groom and had six chefs and four burly waiters to help me if things kicked off. I wasn't going to stand for this crap from a drunk. Thankfully for all concerned our wedding planner came in the nick of time before someone got nicked and 'Phil' backed off. Sybling was on her day off, at their home just across the car park, she re-did the transaction, this time with paper. Her arrival was a calming influence on the groom, as they had met several times during the organising of the day. Finally they left, but no longer happy. A function that went perfectly well so nearly descended onto Meridian news via ITV with a bun fight.

We have had many funeral wakes at the hotel; most of these are obviously sombre affairs, and most are terribly sad; but some are a riot, offering a real party atmosphere for all. Rather than recount my views on the wakes of others, I'll use my own experiences of a wake held at Mortons House, for my father, Maxwell Edward Hageman.

My brother Gavin had found the location for the burial, strictly as per my father's instructions, which were very detailed. It would be a woodland burial site, so we'd get to plant a tree. No sermon, song or prayer, my Pop also wanted a cardboard coffin and asked us to plant an oak tree. If we wanted to waste money, he said in his will, we should have a party afterwards. That party was to be at my hotel, quite close to Blandford and the burial site. Surely I could vouch for the place and the food.

When we arrived at the hotel after the burial, we filed into the Oak Room, where there was no champagne chilling as I had asked. Apparently we were twenty minutes earlier than I'd said, and calling in advance had done nothing to help. The champagne was finally poured a little warmer than preferable and we toasted the life of my now buried father. I hadn't been close to him until my parents separated in the mid-eighties, but now I realised that after 38 years of relying on him and his wisdom I would suddenly have to do without him. The hearse got stuck in the mud in Blandford and that just about summed my dad up, late for his own funeral. The mud covering the guys from the funeral directors as they tried to free their stricken motor was the icing on the cake, if not the cardboard box.

The buffet had been specifically designed to suit all those present – people with and without teeth, vegetarian and carnivore, the fussy and the easy-to-please, the more and less sober, and Pop's grandchildren – our kids Jemma and Emily. I had ordered carefully. The head chef was very busy that day, so the job was left to our number three, a chef de partie nicknamed 'Max.' He was big on heart, if a little lacking in passion and ambition, but I never realised he was almost completely talentless until that day. I was not hugely surprised to see that the four choices of sandwiches I'd specified were translated to cheese and pickle, cheese and onion, cheese and tomato and cheese and cucumber. No chicken, no ham, no salmon, no beef, nor any of the other suggestions I'd made.

A selection of vol au vents, some filled with creamed mushrooms or egg and cress for the veggies, were OK, but the ones filled with a prawn cocktail looked just like prawns in tomato ketchup. No one but I seemed to notice, and none of my family would dare to comment, as I was paying, but if this was the standard he could produce for the owner, I wondered what was going out to my paying guests. Even after years in this trade, I was a little surprised that I had been so badly let down, and on this day I had less patience than normal. Spitting nails, I went to the kitchen to talk with 'Max'. Not much was said: I told him how bad it was, and thanked him sarcastically for his 'efforts' that were shockingly bad. He didn't wait for too much more criticism; maybe he knew the dessert was as awful. He left, never to be seen again. And the dessert was *that* bad.

The party guests didn't seem to care, or notice; my brothers and I talked of the good old days, of Pop and holidays; there were stories galore. Some relatives we'd rarely seen listened and added anecdotes from bygone times. Despite the poor showing from a now departed chef, it was a great day to bury my Pop. He would have been proud, as we were to have had the privilege of knowing him.

Only one of the two Max's that I lost that day meant anything to me; unfortunately I learnt too late that he had meant everything.

Photo courtesy of Sonja Kapp

Be kind to your mother-in-law, but pay for her board at some good hotel.

Josh Billings

10

Bragging Rights

"Six double gin and tonics, three large whiskeys, three vodkas with coke and a pack of cards please, all with ice and a slice." "What would 52 soldiers of the Devil want with ice, Olav?" I replied and got a blank look.

"Basil, why don't you join us for a drink and a game of three card brag?"

I responded with a slightly unkind comment, "Haven't you lost enough today already?" Olav had lost his wallet in Swanage earlier that day. It contained cash, credit cards, his ID and, more importantly to me, the hotel door security code and welcome card. It was beyond me to see him both cheerful and about to gamble when he had no money and had lost his identity.

Olav was one of three Norwegian guests staying as part of a group of twelve from around Europe. Corporate guests staying at the Elizabethan manor were no rarity but on this occasion these guys and one gal were the only guests, so I didn't object to their offer but declined to join them.

The group formed an ominous circle outside on the patio by the carp pond, which was now surrounded by sharks of the card playing variety. The new anti-smoking laws weren't popular with these guys because they were forced outside so as not to be disturbed during their game.

Gambling on licensed premises is prohibited unless a special licence is gained. But in the depths of Dorset and with no other residents I would turn a blind eye, as Gunnar and Olav told me that the stakes would be low and, as they all worked for the same corporation, knew the score.

The plumes of cigarette smoke above the table and orders for drinks became more and more regular; along with the pleadings from the group for the Innkeeper to join them. Despite having seen notes bearing the name of my Queen piled high on the table meaning the stakes had clearly increased dramatically, I took out a bottle of gin, whiskey and vodka, some mixers and took my seat at the table along with Sybil's petty cash tin. I was intent on playing it low and slow so as not to risk the wrath of the trouble and strife in the morning. In fact I could almost feel her anger before losing my first hand with a good pair of Jacks.

Winning hands steeple from three cards with no pairs but the highest card counts, to a pair, a flush where the three cards are the same suit, a run where the cards are different suits, a running flush and the best hand, a prial, when all three cards are the same number, Aces being tops.

I was never stupid enough to be more than £100 down at anytime but rarely found myself in front. I was now one of the chain smokers and my bravado increased as my personal bottle of Rioja emptied. The group had agreed that we would deal the last hand at 1:00am. sharp, I just prayed my non-PC decision to play wouldn't mean the emptying of the PC-tin. The problem was the Ante or opening stake had risen to £10 and the group were now betting in bundles and some were going 'blind' too. Not looking at their cards meant a big risk, but those that had peaked were forced to bet double. I saw the wisdom in looking but paid the price a couple of times. The other important thing to remember is this, if you have looked at your cards, you cannot 'see' or call a 'blind man'. So you have to continue or fold your cards.

The sodium floodlights illuminated the courtyard and our game just sufficiently to continue but candles from the restaurant were added to improve visibility and the atmosphere, as we headed towards the curfew. I replenished the spirits from the bar and re-took my seat at a table with another bottle of Rioja. I was starting to wish I had ignored the invitation. The cards were not falling for me, and when I thought they were, 'a blind man' took my money with his luck.

As the bewitching hour approached I reckoned my pot was now about £80 lighter than when I 'stole' Sybil's pot and I had also smoked a month's supply of cigarettes. Despite this I recharged the glasses and we prepared for the final hand. There were five players left including me, three Norwegians Olav, Gunnar and Magnus and a Catalonian called Marti. It appeared at first glance that most of the players had similar pots to play in the curtain closer.

It was my turn to deal, so nervously I dealt three cards to each player. Griping pains of fear now struck me, as I knew money was little object to these rich men on expense accounts. I had seen the way they bet, sometimes laying down £100 before looking at their cards. Then they might bluff a few hundred more and see off the Innkeeper who showed his face of fear only too clearly before folding his hand.

True to form the Norwegians all opened the betting with a £40 'blind' bet. Marti followed, but I couldn't risk having my marital rights suspended by Sybil or indeed my personal tools dismembered had I lost the contents of the hotel float. So I peeled back my cards one by one, the first card was a two, followed by another. So I had a low pair, not something I would 'go to town' with and bet my lot. Trying not to let my face tell a story I started peeling back the last card, it was another two. That was a great hand, three of a kind, a prial, not something we had seen before that night, nor had I ever been dealt with in my life. While it was the lowest prial, I knew I could bet and bet big.

As the only 'open' player at the table my stake was £80, double my opponents. Round after round we continued at this rate before Gunnar raised to £50 blind, I continued, but now at £100 a round.

Suddenly I started to sweat, the realisation had dawned that as the hotel proprietor this was not a hand I should win. I had no licence to gamble, these guests would lose more heavily because it was the last hand, and worse, I had dealt it! I was clearly looking uncomfortable when the normally quiet and polite Catalunian asked me if things were getting a bit too hot for me. This was my first opportunity to ask my fellow gamblers to fold. They laughed, and laughed long and loud at me. They saw my feeble attempt to force the issue as a bluff. Marti immediately raised the stakes to £100 blind and my heart sank as I emptied the last notes from Sybil's tin to respond. A moment enjoyed by everyone but me.

After removing a wad of cash from the hotel safe, my wallet and the days cashing up folder, I was now determined, scared, and also a little panicked because I was expecting to win despite worrying over the consequences if I failed. I made one last effort to get the guys to look at their cards by saying I had done my best to warn them they were likely to lose and that they must suffer the losses and not bleat afterwards. This had only minimal effect, the Norwegians and my tormentor Marti looked at their cards. Magnus folded having seen nothing not to smile about. A few more rounds of betting took the stake to £200 a go, before I made my move. Raising my bet to £500 brought a sudden silence to those in our den of iniquity. Not because of my bet, but because a member of the local constabulary was standing behind my left shoulder, unseen by me. He had silently watched my raising stake placed in a pile of notes running into thousands of pounds.

His opening words were "Is Olav Gunnerson among this group?" Olav stood looking almost as frightened as me. The copper then said "I have your wallet, Sir. It was handed into the station an hour ago, so I thought I would drop it off on my way home." Followed by, "Can I have a word please, Mr. Hageman?" Being drunk, at first I wondered how he knew my name, but as I sobered up quickly I realised that it is displayed above the front door as all licensees names are and he was our local copper.

I left the table and approached the rotund constable. He made it clear to me that I was skating on thin ice by allowing my property to be used for the purpose of illicit gambling. I protested that the game had started with a few coppers per hand and had gotten out of control, pleading that this would be the last hand and it would never happen again. The policemen said he'd contact me in the morning to discuss the situation and as he left told those seated at the table that this hand must be the last.

As he disappeared from sight the gambling stopped. My huge raise in the stake and the sight of the local Bobby had deflated the atmosphere and the egos of my opponents. All of them seemed happy to call me and see what my fussing was all about.

It was a close run thing; Olav had a running flush, Gunnar a flush and Marti a pair of kings. The reason they had been betting so much was that each of them had hands that would win most games we had played that night. To get dealt hands like these on the final deal was astonishing. That thought bounced into my mind like a basketball fired from a canon into a squash court. Would they think I had rigged the deck before dealing?

I turned over my cards one by one to the stunned silence. To my relief I was congratulated by all of them and nobody cast a dodgy eye, drew a gun or pointed finger at the jubilant but green coloured innkeeper. I chose to count my winnings after the group had filed off to bed talking in whispers as they went.

I repaid the petty cash tin and Sybil's takings folder for the day and refilled the safe and my wallet; the amount I stuffed into my trousers was a little over £3500. I separated about £400 from this to give to Sybil to add more to her shoe mountain in the hope that inflating her Imelda Marcos sized collection might get me off the hook for risking everything. She has never had any idea how much I won that night (unless she reads this).

A sleepless night followed for Basil, as I felt sure the losers would round on me or if they didn't Sybil would, and then there was the policeman to deal with.

Olav and Gunnar came to breakfast first. They shook my hand and said nothing about the game when staff came close enough to hear about the shenanigans of the night before. When I said I was concerned about sore losers getting even, they laughed and said that had the copper not turned up they would have bet much more. Both said they wouldn't have warned other players of an almost unbeatable hand, but they were glad that I had! Marti confirmed this view when he arrived full of smiles but with an empty wallet.

Sybil seemed full of it and was trawling the Internet for a load of cobblers fare before the group checked-out. That just left the fat constable to worry about.

To this day, his flat feet have never come back through the manor house door, but the fear of him doing so has prevented me trying to repeat the feat.

I may have had plenty to brag about, but unusually chose not to, as it wasn't an altogether proud moment. But when my fifteen minutes of inevitable fame was doubled to thirty as Ted and I appeared on National television in front of 4 million viewers, I wanted everybody to know.

11

Making a Show of Yourself

"All the world's a stage" some literary bloke once wrote and, by golly, he was right! It's one of those things and the fatal attraction of being in the hotel business. You may not be treading the boards of Broadway but you can be a star in your own firmament. Deep down inside, the ham in me or, since I aim to run a classy joint, perhaps the jambon en gelée reine pédauque, will out. A yearning to see my name in lights or before the public eye and preferably not on a "wanted" poster.

The BBC had found a formula for a programme that would consume a minimal part of their budget, called "Ready, Steady, Cook." The show involved two contestants bringing in a different shopping bag full of ingredients unknown to the chefs. They range from a 'Budget' bag with goods costing £5, a 'Bistro' bag at £7.50, or, if you're lucky, a 'Gourmet' bag at £10. Contestants then tip the bags out on the counter and the chefs get twenty minutes to make a three-or-more course meal out of the contents. During this time the 'mad-as-a-hatter' host, Ainsley Harriet, asks about the contestant's lives and hears anecdotes, both personal and professional. For the price of a grocery shopping basket, they've got themselves a programme.

Being in the business, at 4:30pm every weekday I sit and watch "Ready, Steady, Cook!" on BBC2.

One afternoon, just as the programme credits were rolling, I heard an invitation for people to audition to appear on the show. I thought this would be a great opportunity – imagining Ted versus Andy, and so north versus south, short versus tall, brawn versus brains, handy versus handsome.

I downloaded the entry forms from the programme's website. Ted and I filled them in and posted them off. He agreed that it was a good opportunity and likely to be fun. We made clear on our applications that we wanted to appear together on the show, and cook against each other.

A couple of months had passed and we had forgotten about the possibility of appearing on television, when one afternoon I got a call from one of the production team asking us to attend an audition in Bristol. After a three-hour drive, we found our way to the designated hotel. We registered at reception and waited in the "Ready, Steady, Cook!" holding room. As we weren't stars already, this wasn't green.

There were about a dozen other hopefuls being grilled by the production team. We all answered some probing questions and discussed aloud what we thought we were good and bad at, all on camera. Then there was a quick-fire round of food related questions. "What animal product does an ovo-vegetarian eat?" one of the researchers asked me. I guessed at eggs and was right. After our twenty minutes in front of a handy cam, it was over and we headed off for another three bum-numbing hours in the car back to the Isle of Purbeck.

We got a call some months later from Stephen Flynn from Endemol Television, who make the programme for the BBC, asking us for our choice of one of three dates to film the show. We picked our date and waited for the letter of confirmation. When it arrived, it noted who our chefs would be. There are about ten chefs that work the show and we were asked on our original applications who we would prefer. Because we had set the battle on a north versus south theme, Ted chose Brian Turner as his celebrity chef, and I chose

Antony Worrall Thompson. Ted was lucky and got his man, but mine was from even further north – Nick Nairn is from Scotland. I liked the way he cooked, having seen him many times on the show. I knew he had a fine dining restaurant, so I wasn't upset at all, despite the accent.

Most of the celebrity chefs have their own restaurants, their income is supplemented by turning on the style and getting in an occasional plug on air. This was something Ted and I were prepared to do – getting our hotel's name and perhaps its website address on a major UK television channel with 4 million viewers couldn't be bad for business or our egos. That ham thing again.

As Ted and I had an award-winning restaurant we were given identical 'Gourmet' bags. These contained venison, onion, potato, leeks, carrots, parsnip, a Bramley apple, and a large piece of Dorset Blue Vinney, which was donated by the hotel's cheese supplier.

We were allowed to take only two guests each; I took Sybil, my brother Paul, and his wife Sharan. As Ted's relatives lived too far north and would need a passport to come this far south, he took only Sybling.

My brother had done a smashing deal for us all to stay at the Ritz in London, where we got £480 per night rooms for £100. We were greeted at the door by the concierge and shown to our rooms after checking in. I wasn't prepared to change into a jacket and tie to take afternoon tea, nor was I warned that it wasn't possible to enjoy most of the ground floor without them. Sybling and Ted felt the same but they went across the road to Costa Coffee to enjoy a cigarette. I gave up afternoon tea for room service and a pre-TV bath.

When we arrived by taxi for the filming of the show, Ted and I were a little nervous. But all the planning had been done and we were well looked after. Ainsley put us at ease with a few jokes. He was, as ever, confident about the show, and about us, or so he said. First I was ushered upstairs to the director and sound engineers.

When filling out my application form, under the section asking for the 'craziest thing you have ever done', I put, 'attempt to break the world record for the loudest whistle (just failing by .2 of a decibel)'. That was never likely to be overlooked, as they made me whistle at the audition, but I was half hoping it might be, though, giving us more time to name-drop the hotel in the programme at every given opportunity. I was asked to "Give it a go, to test the microphones." I did, and blew every radio microphone in the room. I was the only one who thought that was funny.

In the studio, after being powder-puffed by the makeup girl, we were ready. No sooner had it started than it was over. I had just two moments I try to forget; one was knocking over a bottle of olive oil in a rush, the other when I was asked to whistle by Ainsley, just after eating a large chunk of Blue Vinney. I managed to whistle out a few lumps of the mouldering cheese while attempting to blow the mikes again, but it was a blast.

I was very happy with 'my' chef Nick Nairn – indeed my performance on camera. Ted didn't have quite the same luck, as Brian Turner seemed intent on being on camera as much as he could, at the expense of sensible comments or cooking. Nick and I won by a street, with many more 'Red Tomato' vote cards held up by the judges, who were also the audience. Once the show ended, the contestants and their guests get some photo and autograph opportunities and then are expected to eat the food prepared for them by the chefs. Much to the delight of the crew but the dismay of the production team, we had booked dinner elsewhere at the Aubergine in Chelsea and left them to finish the meals we left behind. They don't get many perks at the BBC.

At the Aubergine, the then general manager, Thierry Tomasin, greeted us. He also treated us like royalty. He is sommelier extraordinaire whom I met first when he trained the staff at my hotel. Tonight, though, he was a friend and host. We almost exclusively chose the 'menu gourmand,' a tasting menu of many courses. Sybil and Sybling were more specific and chose from the à la Carte menu. The Aubergine chef, William Drabble, produced a food experience beyond even our dreams: it was exceptional in every way. My personal favourites were the seared scallops, with velouté of Jerusalem artichokes as a starter and the poached lobster tail with a cauliflower purée and caviar that followed. The flavours either exploded in our mouths as they should have or announced themselves quietly when required to, like the wives' sea bass did, with its parsley and olive crust. Thierry matched every course with the perfect wine, which prevented us making a mistake.

After too many bottles of wine and digestifs, we returned to the Ritz so plastered that we shouldn't have been allowed in. However, we didn't really misbehave until we got upstairs. Silly juvenile things that two fortysomethings – one my brother, the other my brother-in-law – shouldn't have done because they knew better! Still, then I was a thirtysomething, and could at least say that I was young enough to hell raise with some kind of justification. We caused no damage and made no mess, but we ran up and down our floor ringing the doorbells of all the rooms, just the sort of thing that would turn me all Basil if it were guests at the Elizabethan manor house. Once our wives had told us off, we settled into emptying the mini-bars of alcohol. The funniest sight was Ted hiding in the blanket box at the end of their bed while Sybling went to our room to empty the mini-bar, he was the only one small enough to fit in the thing. He then jumped out at her when, she returned with armfuls of miniature spirits. My miniature partner was already full of high spirits with more to follow.

We were told that our show would be screened on January 27th 2004 at 4:30 p.m. on BBC2. Of course we told our families, many favourite customers, suppliers and some friends – only to be informed early that month that we had been moved to the 28th. Another set of advices went out to all we knew and we advertised the change on our website.

January 28th started with a buzz around the whole hotel, guests and staff alike. It had become apparent around 2:00 p.m. that the BBC2 afternoon schedule was being altered dramatically by the findings of Lord Hutton. He had a lot to say about weapons of mass destruction, Iraq and Tony Blair, but unfortunately nothing about "Ready, Steady, Cook!"

We got a call from Endemol at about 3.50pm, when Stephen Flynn told us that the show had been dropped in favour of more from the good Lord. We were told it would be rescheduled for sometime in the summer. We had, of course, no time to call the thousands of people we had advised, who would be waiting to see our 30 minutes of fame. The other 4 million viewers we planned to tell about Mortons House Hotel would have to wait too.

A couple of weeks later, my mobile telephone rang as I walked with my family along Las Ramblas in the Catalonian capital, we were there mainly to overcome the sudden death of my father and prepare for his funeral. The caller was Stephen Flynn. The programme had been found a slot for the following day. This left no time to inform the departed guests and friends who wanted to watch us, nor any professional colleagues. Not even our website man could be persuaded to work that fast. I missed my own television debut, sadly so had my father, my proud wife and our two daughters. We had to settle for watching it on tape on our return. It wouldn't be the same not watching it 'live' and knowing that we were among the many guests and friends that missed it – but millions of others didn't.

When we collected the tape and sat at home to watch the show, the kids were very excited. The prospect of seeing Daddy on television seemed more important to them than to me. We came across well enough, I thought, and we didn't look too nervous. The editors managed to cut most of my continual mentions of the hotel and its website address, despite us doing the show in one take, but we got the name across enough times to notice the benefits with bookings.

To my relief no one could see lumps of Blue Vinney flying from my mouth at 116 decibels an hour, give or take a whistle or two.

I framed the photos that were hastily taken on the day, along with my wife's autographed voting card and my Blue-Vinney-stained red tomato apron. It has pride of place in my kitchen at home reminding me of my glory day and the half hour of fame that I had missed

Ah, the smell of the greasepaint, the roar of the crowd – or is it the other way round?

The only other times I have cooked for 'show' is when I became The Great Zabaglione for charity.

Sybil had taken me to a hotel in Brockenhurst with the kids to enjoy a short break in a Spa hotel, with a restaurant not dissimilar to mine. Unfortunately, the receptionist neglected to tell us when we booked that under-16s couldn't use the pool – no fun when your pre-teenage daughters travel with swimsuits in their luggage.

One night, the girls fancied somewhere a little less formal for dinner. We found a local restaurant called "Il Palio 2", a highly recommended Italian restaurant and pizzeria. We had a great meal that tasted authentic – the staff even looked vaguely Italian. I had enjoyed the house cannelloni, and the girls all had pizzas. On the dessert menu, I saw my choice immediately; Zabaglione is a very big favourite of mine.

The reason Zabaglione takes so long to deliver to the expectant guest is that it usually requires a real chef to make it to order, as amateurs often come up with scrambled eggs. Rarely in this country can you get a good one. If the restaurant owner takes your order and returns with a beautiful copper stove to cook it in front of you at the table you are very lucky, especially if you go to "Il Palio 2" by the station. During the performance, I asked my man where he got his 'fire'. He told me in his wonderful accent that you could only get them from Italy – what a surprise! I was feeling confident after my carafe of Montepulciano, so I asked if he could get me one.when he next went home. To my delight he was returning to his hometown the next day, and he agreed to acquire one for me. I never truly expected him to honour his offer though.

A week later, while I was travelling down the M3, my mobile rang. It was Signor Palio himself: "Mr Andy, I have'a your fire." A detour to Brockenhurst was easy – not so the invoice for 300 euros! He asked me why I wanted it so badly and joked that being an Englishman I'd never make a Zabaglione using it, especially without a proper recipe. Luckily, I had not been completely sloshed a week or so earlier and I tried to remember exactly what he had put into the copper pan and in what order. When I recited this back to him, his mood improved and he gave me his recipe in full. I asked him where I could get a quality copper pan, and he gave me one of his, from the wall. I also left with a bottle of Cremovo Marsala to start me off, again on him. Good chap.

I had no idea then that I would go on to use my stove to such effect. After some nervous practice at home, I decided it was time to go for broke at the hotel; the reason was "Children in Need." I would cook and serve Zabaglione for two at the table for a minimum donation of £10, all proceeds going to Children in Need via Mr. Wogan. The fund-raising marathon of a show is broadcast on BBC television and takes place on a Friday night. Even in November the hotel was full for the weekend – we had 30 diners booked in the restaurant. I had prepared to serve about half of these; the others either hated the thought of it, or despised naff charity beggars like me.

I was shattered by the end of the evening, having cooked 22 Zabagliones. Thanks to Signor Palio, his fire and his recipe, there were none that resembled scrambled eggs as he had gloomily predicted – easily done, if you are not careful. The hotel had lost out on the revenue from the dessert orders but costs were minimal, just a few egg yolks, some white wine, cremovo and sugar, whisked into a Sabayon over the flame. The pastry chef was delighted at only having to do a few puddings (he hates it when I call them that). I raised £400 for the charity, as some customers donated more than the minimum, for the theatre of it. I sent a picture postcard off to Brockenhurst to let them know of my success.

My stove was retired to the dumb waiter (no, not Manuel) until a worthy customer deserved a show or a dumber waiter offered a Zabaglione to someone I didn't know. When the 'fire' came out this always attracted ridicule from the chefs, who hate it if the boss can cook, unless they are short-handed, but more so if the dish is popular. We did put Crepes Suzette on the menu partly to use my 'fire' and because it was real theatre – although for these performances I relied upon the skills of restaurant staff.

My next outing for charity was for Comic Relief. As a seasoned performer, I was better prepared for more customers this time, and I had been collecting donations from now departed guests in the weeks prior to the big day.

On the night itself, if all went well I'd raise £500 I hoped. I feared the worst – which would be too many orders coming too quickly. The pastry chef had prepared my ingredients, even melting Valrhona chocolate and decorating the inside of the glass serving bowl with a wacky pattern, then putting them in the freezer, awaiting my call. Sybil's hairdresser Calina had got me a decent supply of red hair spray paint. My hands and shoes were decorated with the signal red noses of the year and I wore my Red Nose Day 05 T-shirt with pride. I looked shocking – comically so, which was the whole idea. I think I showed off my green "Ready, Steady, Cook!" apron too, which clashed perfectly.

It was hard work, but after 37 personally made Zabagliones cooked in the theatre and style of Signor Palio, I had raised £635 for Comic Relief; the certificate to prove it is displayed in my office. Many photographs appeared with the news on our website; a few were sent to absent sponsors, some to appease and others to thank, in case I had cajoled too hard. I even got a thank you letter from Comic Relief. An e-mail from one guest just said "A real clown."

Satisfied with the other charitable causes the hotel supports, I thought that enough was enough. However my daughters felt differently and persuaded me that we should again put on another 'show'. Only this time the girls designed my outfit and hairstyle. They also set me the target of £1000 to raise for the Children in Need appeal on Friday in November 2006.

Their idea was that I would look a little like Pudsey the bear, but despite the intended colour, as depicted on the tin of hairspray, when it came out it was distinctly lime green! The styling was very much the kid's idea and was popular with most. Cooking the desserts on two separate occasions in the now famous outfits this time I raised £956.50, a little short of Jemma and Emily's target, but I was still very happy, if a little exhausted. It gets harder and harder to raise money for charity, however worthy the cause, I try very hard to inject some humour into the events and have succeeded this time, certainly. Although some thought I looked more like Sid Vicious than a cuddly bear with custard coloured hair.

One of the chefs offered to make good the difference in monies raised to reach the £1000 target if I was willing to shave off all my hair. Needless to say I politely declined, having put my hair and the customers through enough already!

That may just be it, for the hair-raising fundraiser.

But there's no business like show business.

However, the most hair raising event any hotel proprietor can have is with some of his guests, guests who appear to have arrived straight from Hell.

12

Guests from Hell

Hotels like mine don't win awards, or stay in business if the guests are unhappy. If you have read this far you may find it hard to take my word for it, but please try. Writing endless accounts of guests that ooze praise while paying their accounts would be boring. So those that follow are my favourite disgruntled guests from Hell. It's my top ten chart, for out of the ten thousand guests we have entertained each year, a mere 0.1% have been unhappy campers. It is possible in some cases that they are from a different planet and it is unlikely that they will be back, not that they will be invited by Basil or Sybil.

At number ten – The Graffiti Artist

Whoever said the English don't complain was wrong, or maybe times have changed. The Yanks have taught us well. Sometimes guests act as many English people used to though, and say nothing when things aren't going well, which leaves us no opportunity to make things right once they have departed. Some write to us later, but one couple had their own novel idea, one I had not seen before.

After a particularly boozy Saturday night, the couple in Room 14 rang down to reception at 10:45am and demanded a cooked breakfast in the room. My receptionist claimed the hangover was audibly detectable on the phone.

We stop taking cooked breakfast orders in the restaurant at 9:30

a.m. in order to get ready for the busy Sunday luncheon trade, although we continue serving continental breakfasts in the bedrooms until 10:00 a.m. We declined the demand from room 14, because we had 60 people dining later for Sunday lunch, so today wasn't the day to bend the rules. We offered them some tea and coffee and biscuits in the bar and we also reminded them that checkout was 11:00 a.m.

It is possible to arrange a later checkout if the hotel is not full that night, but unlikely when you are rude to the receptionist. They clearly chose to use the remaining minutes of their stay to deface the guest information folder in the room, with delicacies of a very offensive nature. Writing comments under our information which is put there to help the guest experience. Offering their own advice to future guests such as; "Beware Basil, he walks around the hotel like he owns the place jangling a bunch of keys big enough to be a jailors. Play by his rules and it will feel like a prison."

Not so bad, I guess: I have read and said nastier things; but worse if another guest reads the comments – embarrassing, too, because the writer dated his work. Worse still, though, if the graffiti is brought to your attention four months later by a 'spoon salesman.'

At number nine – Enough to make you sick in the wallet
Room 16 – The Purbeck Suite – with Jacuzzi and lounge area, overlooking the steam railway and pond

A guest checked out of the Purbeck Suite without uttering a word when paying, a little late on a Sunday afternoon. It's an outside room, one the housekeepers do last, finishing it maybe by 2.00 p.m., the theoretical check-in time for the next occupants. When the girls opened the door, they were overwhelmed by a stench too putrid to describe – puke! At the end of a long day and with twenty other bedrooms checking out, this was all they needed. Some fool at reception then gave them permission to leave it until Monday, as it wasn't let later that day. The room stewed as I festered at the news.

The guest, who hadn't eaten in the hotel the night before and clearly didn't feel like breakfast, had vomited throughout the suite of rooms. It was almost as if he had employed a team to vomit with him as there were not neat piles everywhere, it was spread around. I cannot describe the stench or the mess, because it was that bad. The room had to be 'blocked off empty' for three days, meaning it wouldn't get sold. Whilst the room was stripped from top to bottom so that every component part could be cleaned, laundered and more, I set about finding the man who had done this and said nothing, leaving as if it was normal to do so without a word when checking out.

Firstly, under the 'umbrella' of several disclaimers placed around the hotel, on our tariff and displayed on the website, I deducted what amounted to cleaning fees, room rates (at 75%) and expenses totalling £700 from his credit card. Having used it once, it was easy and legal to add another charge. The notices around the hotel explained that we would recover, in any way we could, the costs of guests' negligence or damage – without any further notice.

The room was actually out of action for four days, because we could still smell puke, so we replaced the carpet and underlay and then debited some more money and sent him the bill. The man called and demanded an explanation and sounded really pissed off, but strangely when I drew his attention to the notices on our tariff and guest information, in his room and at reception, along with that on our website, he calmed down. When he said that he'd recover his money in court, I calmly let slip that we had photographs of every pile of vomit he had left behind him and would willingly show them in court. In addition he had used the iron but not the ironing board, he left the iron still on, face down on the carpet, and we took pictures of this too. We never heard from him again, which was a surprise, he seemed up for a fight, but then maybe, just maybe, he'd accepted that the damage was his responsibility – or was it just that he had been away with someone else and left his partner at home?

Accidents happen; damage innocently caused and reported is often overlooked. I could never overlook anything like this as it falls below the level of normal decency expected of guests. The level is dropping though!

Coming in at number eight – The Hotel Lush

One December night, the hotel was strangely quiet; somehow the date had been overlooked for office Christmas parties. The restaurant still had 22 diners and we had only four rooms vacant. As a young blonde lady was checking-in she made it known to me that she was racing the following day in Weymouth. Her father was a former powerboat champion and she wanted to follow in his wake – if you see what I mean. She seemed pleasant enough, if a little over-confident that her looks counted for something. She told me on the way to the room that her taxi driver had said our chefs spend more time on presentation than the cooking, so I was surprised when she booked a table for dinner in the a la Carte restaurant.

When she came to the bar I was serving another guest. She interrupted our conversation and demanded a hot chocolate, telling me that even in a budget hotel there was always complimentary hot chocolate supplied in the bedroom. I finished pouring the drinks for a nice couple and ended my conversation with them. I turned to the bombshell and explained that we don't get asked for hot chocolate often and therefore supply organic tea, green tea, caffeine-free fruit teas and speciality coffees in all the rooms. We also leave packets of biscuits in addition to the fresh cookies that are made daily by the pastry chef and placed in the cookie jars. I also mentioned that I could make her a fresh hot chocolate using frothed milk from our cappuccino machine, when she was ready for it. I never said this would be chargeable before she shouted at me, "The customer is always right, or don't you know that!"

When she had taken her seat in the bar, I delivered her Rum and Coca Cola and gave her menus and a wine list.

She decided against the a la Carte menu, choosing instead a Rib eye steak and a Pomme Pont-Neuf from the lounge menu. She asked for some tomato ketchup and a special cream and peppercorn sauce to be made to accompany her beef, which she wanted very well done. I was surprised at this because she was a self-proclaimed foodie and these rarely want cremated beef. Maybe she was swayed by the arrival of another single male guest who was dining in the bar. They seemed to be pairing up.

When her meal arrived, her mobile telephone rang at the table and she ignored the waitress while she answered it. The call lasted at least fifteen minutes, during which time no staff could approach to ascertain if things were to her liking. When I finally got the chance, she complained at having only seven chips and that when at MacDonald's she could get 70 chips for 99p. I immediately offered to get her some more, but knowing it would take time as these were no ordinary chips and were made to order. She asked me to re-heat her steak and make some more sauce for its return.

When I came back with her meal, I tried to explain that a Pomme Pont-Neuf is a tower of nine chips; the gaps between each chip look a little like the famous Parisian bridge. She didn't listen or seem to care, but continued with her attack saying she had not been asked if everything was all right by a waiter. I was now in the mood to put her straight. I told her that if she were used to staying in budget hotels that supplied packets of hot chocolate in every room, she would most likely find one near a MacDonald's restaurant. If it would make her happier, I would willingly find her alternative accommodation. She wasn't listening, but chose to play with her blonde hair seductively for the man opposite, or so I thought.

Nothing seemed to perturb her; she continued her quest to pull the young man also eating in the bar. Her antics obviously impressed him, as they soon left for the local pub. I finished my restaurant walkabout, talking to proper customers, and retired to my office upstairs to finish the day's paperwork. At around 11:00 p.m. the 'couple' returned to the hotel with a noisy and drunken bravado. The young man sensibly went to bed, leaving the girl to stagger up to my office door. As I lifted eyes from the computer screen, denim greeted them! The girl had lifted her leg onto my desk so that her crotch was inches from my nose; she then tried to tell me that she needed my help or a doctor. Now she was flirting overtly, but this time at me, she told me that somehow she had super-glued her jeans to her leg when trying to fix her racing helmet.

She was desperate for my 'help' and a suggested remedy. She even said she would do anything to get her jeans off and anything after she had!

I thanked God Sybil didn't walk into the office at that moment as she would not have seen the funny side of my proximity to the blonde's 'nunnie'. Basil slipped passed her and her fluttering eye lashes to get her some washing-up liquid, I returned to find her reclining seductively in my chair in the office. I told her to take a hot bath before massaging the affected area with the liquid soap before trying to remove her jeans. I also told her I wouldn't help her do it. I was relieved when she left the office, looking rather forlornly as the twenty something blonde had failed to hook the hotelier two decades her senior, to do something she had been trying all night – get her jeans off.

Number seven in the charts – In the Shit

This was not really a guest from Hell but a guest who endured a fate somewhat worse than death. Room 10 – A double room with a castle view

A delegate attending a BP course at another hotel but staying with us arrived just as we had started to serve dinner. She declined the opportunity to join other diners in the restaurant and was shown to her room. Miss Jordan came back to reception a few minutes later and complained that the toilet in her bedroom was blocked. Unusual and untimely as the restaurant was busy and I was needed to help the front of house team. It was a job Ted would have dealt with if it occurred during the day, but I wasn't going to call him across from the cottage for something so simple. Thankfully, the guest agreed to go out for walk, and I asked her to tell reception when she was leaving the hotel and I would solve the simple problem while she was out.

I continued restaurant service until I got a call to reception. The guest had returned and was not happy that I had not lived up to my promise, as her loo was still blocked. As I went upstairs with my industrial toilet plunger, I gave the receptionist a scathing glare. She had forgotten to tell me that the guest had gone out some 40 minutes earlier. I had hoped to be alone when unblocking her toilet, as it can be unpleasant, but she chose to follow me back to the room.

I rolled up my sleeves, put on some pink plastic gloves that Sybil insists on and set to work, expecting the job to take seconds not minutes. However, I encountered a serious blockage and it wasn't pleasing to the nose, so I closed the door leading to the bedroom and continued. To my relief, the toilet was now clear. So I cleaned up, flushed the loo, poured in some nice smelly blue disinfectant and sprayed the bathroom with an industrial-strength tangerine perfume. I thanked the guest for her patience, apologised and left. As I walked down the corridor on my way back to reception, I passed the couple from Room 11 returning from dinner. It never looks good to be seen wearing marigold gloves and a suit whilst holding a toilet plunger, especially if the gloves are pink, I remember thinking at the time.

Just two minutes after I had removed my marigolds, the couple in Room 11 rang reception to say *their* toilet was now blocked. I checked the restaurant to see that all was well, accompanied by the pungent smell of disinfectant, before returning upstairs to my stricken guests. Once inside the bedroom, the toilet looked as bad as Miss Jordan's had next door, but just as simple to clear. I apologised to the guests, left them happy and with a waft of pine disinfectant. Just as I closed one door behind me, the next door opened. The woman in Room 10 came out covered in shit. I remember thinking that both she and her mood stank, which wasn't surprising really. Apparently as I was plunging next door, she was sitting on her freshly cleaned toilet going 'about her business' when, she explained, "The toilet just exploded all over me covering me in... well... SHIT!"

The corporate trade often gives me the shits, unfortunately this time I had given some back. I booked her a room at another local hotel and allowed her to leave without charge. What else could I do?

The next morning Ted explained that the waste pipes from the toilets in Rooms 10 and 11 are linked. Unless you block the other toilet with a plastic football when plunging, all you achieve is an overflow next door. When he said overflow, that is only when you plunge gently. That would explain the explosion of shit covering poor Miss Jordan. My second audience had watched me ram the plunger in and out like a man possessed – a little showing off of my plunging skills wouldn't do any harm, I thought.

And at six we had Room 9 – What a ceremony for uninvited guests

Room nine is a twin bedded room with views of the slighted castle.

One spring, two bridesmaids had booked a room in the hotel, as the following day the hotel was the location of their best friends wedding. I had taken the booking for a champagne toast before the ceremony and again afterwards – no meal and no overnight guests. It was a simple and profitable deal.

There would be a maximum of 60 guests attending the ceremony, the limit for the Oak Room, its civil wedding licence and our fire certificate.

The bridesmaids were on hand to ensure that the seating plan agreed upon was laid out to their satisfaction. The bride had arranged for a piano to be delivered to the hotel; this would be played when the guests and then the bride and groom gathered for the ceremony, easy.

We didn't need too many staff on duty as it only took two to pour and serve the champagne once the antique settees had been swapped for our banquet chairs. I wasn't expecting to come into work until later for the busy evening restaurant shift. The wedding guests had agreed to leave by 5pm. Money for old rope this, and a nice simple little earner.

Twenty minutes before the ceremony was due to start I got a call from the hotel. Staff had given one flute of champagne to each guest and had run out with plenty of wedding guests left without. I was told that around eighty people were attending the ceremony. The last thing I heard before I goose-stepped to the hotel, was that the bridesmaids had moved the piano in the Oak Room to behind the door, this to allow more chairs to be fitted in. And that they were now using the rear door as access. All this seemed reasonable to the staff, and why not, you might think? They would pour and charge for twenty more glasses of bubbly, and all was good, I was told.

Except that by changing the previously agreed seating plan and moving the 'Joanna' behind the door, the fire exit was now blocked. The room was only licensed to hold sixty people (with access to the fire escape) and I had told the bride this several times, and luckily it was confirmed in writing.

It was about five minutes before I arrived at the hotel. Unfortunately for all concerned, my mood had taken only this long to change. I ran into reception in a rage: Basil was now exposed to 80 previously relaxed guests. Collaring the best man and the two bridesmaids, I explained that there would be a delay to the service while the piano was moved from the fire exit and twenty chairs removed from the Oak Room. There was no point in them arguing with me after I had explained that if the room wasn't rearranged there wouldn't be a wedding at all. I was awful; I had completely lost my temper and self-control. I tugged furiously at the legs of the piano, vainly trying to drag it out of harm's way, not helped by any one of the stunned onlookers. Eventually word got around that unless they wanted the bride to see my 'show', guests would be best employed in helping me or the whole thing would descend further towards a farce. After a few minutes three guests all dressed as penguins, and I, did the job. 60 for the ceremony left twenty outside watching through the windows. By now, I was perspiring plenty and nothing had calmed my temper. It wasn't that I was just being difficult – I wanted a peaceful afternoon at home playing with the kids, not this hassle. If I had let the wedding go ahead in breach of fire regulations and our wedding licence, this would only be fine *if* nothing happened. But if there had been a fire, injury or even death, it would have been *me* that appeared on the news being led away in handcuffs on a charge of manslaughter, not the bride who had changed the goalposts or the bridesmaids who changed the seating plan. Realising I needed to blow off steam, I walked to the dining room which I had assumed was empty and screamed the foulest of obscenities at the top of my voice. This felt really good until I looked up to see the bride sitting with the registrar, having her pre-wedding interview. They both looked up at me with stunned expressions.

Sybil arrived at the hotel; she had been called at home by the receptionist and asked if she would lead me away from further frustration and maybe a padded cell. She joked on the way that it would be great if a psychiatrist checked in at that moment, just as he had thirty years earlier for Mr Fawlty in Torquay.

Into the top five comes - The couple and the roll top bath

At reception one morning, I took a call and a booking from a lady from Poole, unremarkable except for her insistence that she have the Victoria Room, with the roll-top bath.

Just as I was confirming the details back to her, she stopped me and asked, "I ought to have mentioned earlier and hope you don't mind or have any objections to, or discriminate against..."

"Just ask me, madam, what is it?" I interrupted.

"We are a 'same sex couple' – is that a problem?" I told the lady that there was no problem and she would not be made to feel in the least bit uncomfortable, or indeed noticed.

Some weeks later, the 'couple' checked in and, yes, you guessed it, I was at reception. One woman was beautiful, elegant and feminine, a real stunner I thought, the other had a 'number one' squaddy cut and earrings in every possible place on her face and possibly piercings elsewhere. The ladylike one had a suitcase, or overnight bag; her friend had merely a rucksack. I checked them into the room and showed them all the facilities, adding that the bath filled more quickly than expected and to be careful; also that the Molton Brown non-foaming bath salts were a great relaxant and even if used carefully could put a bull to sleep. The 'lad' grunted that sleep wasn't a part of their plan; I felt myself go a little red and left them to it.

An hour later, there was a desperate call to reception from the girls in the Victoria Room; we quickly ascertained that they needed me in the room, 'sharpish like'. They had put the two-foot-long solid brass plug into the bath and turned on the taps, but they had turned on one tap a bit hard and couldn't turn it off! A panic had ensued and as they tried to lift the huge plug in such a hurry that they had jammed it. Water at mains pressure was gushing out of the huge tap and there was no time to waste, as the water level was within an inch of the top. I arrived in the room seconds later and tried hard to turn it off – without success: I just wasn't man enough. So I wrenched at the plug, just getting it out in time, just before the water overflowed and poured through to the newly decorated Castle Room below. Now that I had time, I was able to use a huge monkey grip on the tap and turn it off, which had become very bloody hot.

My plan was to leave the room, telling them to try and be more careful, but also thanking them for the speed of their call to reception. Then I noticed them trying to cover the things on the bed, which they had not had time to do after calling reception in the panic. To say that there were toys, lubricants and gadgets of pleasure, would be an understatement. I could only imagine what some of them did. But one thing on the bed needed no explanation; it was a huge double-ended latex nob, it was still humming and was probably bigger than the plug that had just caused all the problems.

The look on my face gave away my thoughts. The 'lad' added to my embarrassment with a comment about how satisfying it was to use, and maybe I should watch them. Her partner pulled the covers over her face in embarrassment, although she still laughed. I tried to laugh and left. Each to their own (literally), as long as it doesn't upset others guests, I thought on my way back to reception a lot redder than normal. I don't normally blush, but then that experience and offer were not normal.

At number four in the chart – When I say jump, you jump
Room 21 – (Dackcombe) This accessible room interconnects with room 20.

From the moment he checked in there were nothing but problems. The single guest was not physically disabled – nor would he admit to being spawned in hell or mentally challenged. Staff and I have to handle petty and insignificant complaints very occasionally unless we have no guests. It is part of the job and the business. We comply, repair and serve with a smile that is as securely fixed as pictures are to the walls; but if you really want to you can remove either.

Our new arrival had made a list of complaints and requests written minutes after being taken to his room. He handed this to the receptionist before departing for the rest of the day. He made no friends at reception when he made it clear in a rather curmudgeonly way that all should be complied with before his return. It was difficult to read the list, but harder to comply with. For example, he wanted extra wattage light bulbs put in the bedside lamps, but the ones he wanted exceeded the maximum rating of the lampshade. He left his shoes by the bed and wanted them polished (we offer the polish and brushes but rarely the service, and never to anyone rude). His bedroom laundry bag had been filled and left on the bed – this, he stated, was required by 9:00 a.m. the following morning, but our last laundry collection for 'next day' had passed earlier, at noon.

The other items he listed were easy to deal with and fell within the parameters of our normal service; it was just that no one seemed to want to work from his list. Barbara was called back to the hotel to re-clean his room. "It was not up to the required standards or expectations," she read from his note. He asked if we could remove the previous guest's belongings. There was nothing that Barb needed to do in the room when I inspected it with her.

When he came back to the hotel, he was none too pleased to be told that we couldn't get his laundry back by the time he had asked. The duty manager tried to explain that he would get it back at about 2:00 p.m. the following day – but this was too late for his meeting, he said. She also explained that the light bulbs in his bedside lights were the maximum permitted, and that the housekeepers had placed a standard lamp next to the bed instead. The colour of the face on our guest changed from an angry red to a mad purple. We had tried but failed to live up to his expectations and demands, as he told us when he left for his room, declining the dinner invitation. We all hoped we wouldn't hear from him again until check-out. I was asked to cover the breakfast shift on reception in readiness.

When the occupant of Room 21 came to pay, he did so reluctantly and not without comment. I was ready and willing to take the necessary abuse, but when the guest slammed the bible on the desk, his face distorted in rage, he shouted that a previous guest might be a "God-fearing Christian bible basher," but that *he* didn't want to read the bible this person had left behind him! I thought every guest was aware that every hotel the world over has a Gideon supplied bible in every bedroom.

I remember watching him return to his room after checking-out to collect his belongings, surprised that he hadn't asked for them to be taken to his car. "Good riddance," I mumbled, almost loud enough to be heard – and also something akin to "Why don't you **** off and go to hell."

When Barb and her team went to clean the 'vacant' room (the 'Dackombe' rooms are done last due to their location away from the main hotel), they found our guest slumped on the bed. Lifeless. He had taken me literally. Despite the lack of light from the bedside, our guest had seen enough and departed. To Hell I have no doubt, not that I checked for three 6's behind his ear as he left in a plastic bag. And there's me thinking nobody listens to Basil.

Into the top three with – The Big Tipper and his Spare Pillow
Room 5 is a bedroom in the original building and is not the biggest, but is finished with a beautiful antique Duchess dressing table and an old solid walnut headboard.

Discretion in this trade is a given, although it's often a chore when you have to go beyond the call of duty to hide the shenanigans of some guests. Day-lets are commonplace at most hotels that allow them, this is when the room is required 'during the working day', let's say 11:00 a.m. until 3:00 p.m. at which time the 'couple' check out having paid cash and back to the monotony of less secret lives. When such clandestine goings on are afoot it is often easy to trace the culprits by reading the name on the empty box of 'stay pecker hard pills' in the waist bin next to condom wrappers. Cialis and Viagra induced playtime doesn't come cheap but these folk need to maximise every minute together.

A regular guest, one who always frequented Room 5 with a different 'wife' each time and always requesting during the booking process that we exercise great discretion. He invariably asked for me before he booked, so that he'd be sure to get the message across: it would be awful if you said something like "Good to see you again, sir!" or "Goodness me, madam, you look younger every time I see you!" when you greeted them on arrival.

His lady friends always came in a few minutes after he did and seemed to know the direction to his room. I often wondered at first whether they knew him but I would later discover that they were paid help, or 'spare pillows' as they are known in London – ladies of the night, or in some cases, day, who take up the space in a double bed for reward.

It is very hard when things are busy to be sure you convey the situation to all staff and hope to God that no one fucks up. Regular guests like him who tip well are good for all, I thought at first.

It seemed as if we had played his game a dozen times before, but I was not expecting the frantic call from said gentleman. This time he was asking for my personal help, with the utmost urgency. He explained that his wife was about to enter the hotel through the front door and insisting she "Be stalled there" for as long as it took to get his 'partner' (the hurriedly dressed hooker) out of the room unnoticed.

I thought as quickly as I could before recommending the use of a fire escape close to his room. I ran upstairs and escorted the paid help down the fire escape stairs. This was made more difficult because she hadn't finished becoming 'decent' but Basil had no time to gawp at her expansive bosoms. I reached the relative safety of the ground floor at just the time his wife was being brought up the ornate main staircase (as slowly as possible) by the duty receptionist. It worked like clockwork as she pointed out objects of interest en route. The only person that seemed to suffer was me, heart racing, beads of sweat on my brow, but it would be worth it for the inevitably large tip that he'd leave to be shared by all the staff. I helped the now sultry sex worker out to the A351 amidst protests about the way she had been handled and the fact that she remained unpaid. Not my worry love.

"Sorry if I manhandled you but it was impossible to keep all your bits covered and get you out in a hurry!" All I had to do now was explain to Sybil how I had a cheap aroma of *eau de prostitute* on me.

At check-out the next morning, the bill was paid, and not much was said, none of the usual pleasantries. As it appeared his wife wasn't able to pin anything on him, all was well and I never asked how the wife knew he was at the hotel. Unusually on this occasion he decided not to pay by cash or leave a tip. He either didn't think the years he'd taken off me were worthy of a gratuitous tip, or he wasn't usually generous when he was with his wife.

I was not impressed, but as he left to pack the car, Barb came down with a lipstick that had been left in his room (but not the colour his wife was wearing); so I took it from my housekeeper and rushed out to the car, fuming to myself at the lack of reward for all my efforts and having decided, finally, to end the 'love affairs' the customer had here regularly. I thought of saying "The young lady who left yesterday afternoon left this in the room" but instead bottled it up and I settled for "Would you like a hand loading the car? And please come again!"

I did manage to discreetly palm him the lipstick when shaking hands along with a knowing glare. He never came back. This was not a disappointment, as I have not had to play his game again since. Hidden behind my obsequious smile, there often lie guests' secrets, secrets that people give willingly without a second thought about how well I can be entrusted with them. Ok if you don't misbehave or find Basil having a bad one.

At number two – "Waiter, waiter, there is a fly in my soup"
Room 19 is an accessible room in the walled garden.

Mr. Dent checked in on his own for a four-night 'Hibernation Break' one March. He was unremarkable except for his taste in fine wine. Mr. Dent dined each night, drinking the most expensive wines we had to offer, no expense spared. He was easy to get on with, pleasant even, and popular with staff and owners alike.

On the last morning of his stay, he sat at his table, having helped himself with treats from the breakfast buffet. A few moments later, he loudly shrieked that he'd found mouse droppings in his cereal. As the staff tried in vain to appease him, another guest left the room in a hurry.

What had gone unnoticed by staff, but not the guest who left the dining room, was that Mr. Dent had pulled from his pocket a glass test tube, pouring the contents into his breakfast cereal.

I was at the reception desk when the guest reported to me what he had seen Mr. Dent do; our regular guest even indicated into which jacket pocket the test tube had been returned. I had never heard anything like this before.

Our staff, of course, were mortified and shocked by Mr. Dent's complaint. This was made worse by the volume of his voice, carrying to all corners of the dining room. Staff told me later that they simply didn't know what to do, except apologise and remove all the remaining cereals from the buffet. The remaining guests seemed as stunned, almost to silence, not many ordered anything else, and certainly nobody wanted a breakfast cereal. Most preferring to leave the scene in silence.

Mr. Dent came to reception in a confrontational manner and demanded that I call the local Environmental Health Officer. As I was calmly dialling the imaginary number, the slime ball offered, "To accept a substantial discount to drop the matter." I commented to Mr. Dent that when the Environmental Health Officer arrived, "she might like to see the test tube in your left jacket pocket, from where the droppings came!" Mr. Dent went bright red and even though the red mist descended, he knew I was formidably placed to argue. He packed his bags, paid cash and left.

I helped him to the car with nothing more than a cutting stare. He was blacklisted on our computer, but has never tried to rebook. I don't doubt, though, that he has used this method before then catching out a few hotels less fortunate. He paid cash and therefore we had no idea if Mr. Dent was his real name, but the address he gave us at check-in was false, as was the credit card number to secure the booking. I learnt to get pre-authorisation of all credit cards as a result.

Had a regular guest not seen and reported what had happened, I feel sure that I would have buckled at reception giving the guest his stay for nothing thereby 'Denting' our profits. His wine bill alone was £426; his accommodation was a similar amount. We treated the informant to dinner on us, and thanked him for his honesty. He at least, can still laugh about it when he returns to us each spring. He never orders cereal though.

And topping the list is my favourite, maybe bar one -
Thoroughly Dumped-on.

Room 4 - This is a double-bedded room in the old part of the house, but as it is not very large, it is hard to charge it as a character room. It does have a large bathroom and a wonky window similar to Room 3's, though.

Occasionally the hotel is called upon to play host to travel writers or journalists who intend to 'do a piece' on the Isle of Purbeck.

Often the local Tourist Information Centre contacts us in the first instance, requesting the inevitable 'freebee' in return for a few kind words. Sometimes a 'request' comes in from 'on high' and a regional tourist board asks the question. This time though it was from the very top, the Visit Britain head office in London who made the request, the arrangements and the booking.

Early in the spring of 2006 they had asked me to accommodate a couple for two nights. Mrs. Dumpton was writing for a national newspaper about the many wonders on offer locally but would be accompanied by her husband.

The Tourist board wanted me to provide two nights accommodation and a meal in our fine restaurant, free and gratis. I did not agree lightly or without making very clear to all parties that the hotel should not only feature in the main article but the article should include terms we regard as relevant and important, like 'Small hotel of the Year 2005' or 'Two AA rosette restaurant, Oak panelled drawing room with carvings by Indonesian sailors...Elizabethan manor....' and such like.

On a cold February afternoon the couple checked-in to the double room I had allocated. They were given the usual tour of the ground floor facilities with the receptionist trying hard to feed them possible quotes like "The Oak Room panels were carved by Indonesian sailors..." before being shown to their room. The Dumpton's decided to take a trip into the village centre and to dine in a local pub on the first night, this despite the foul weather. Because of their decision I decided not to work that Sunday evening in preference to a family roast and a robust red at home with my family.

The Dumptons joined in a 'Quiz-night' at The Greyhound Inn staying there all night enjoying the hospitality before returning to the hotel after last orders at the pub. As all the other guests had departed to their beds, the staff decided to lock up the reception desk and bar and get an 'early' night. When guests are shown around the hotel during the check-in tour and on the way to their bedrooms they are asked to take their room key and Welcome Card with them if they expect to return late. They are also advised to take the Welcome Card with them that details many things but importantly the number for the key code entry pad on the front door, useful if you return to find it locked.

Our freeloading journalist and her husband had neither taken their room key or the Welcome Card with them. Fortunately for them there was another couple returning at the same time (with their key code and room key) and through them gained entrance to the hotel. Unfortunately there was no room key visible and no staff to help the Dumptons get into their bedroom. It was what happened next that singled out the Dumptons for their top spot in Guests from Hell.

Guests stranded at reception or indeed outside the hotel are a rarity; most listen to the check-in procedure and take with them what they might need on their return. Some can read after a trip to the pub and most can see one of the two telephones to call night/duty staff. The first phone is situated outside the main door with bright red writing on it that says 'Night/Emergency Phone' with instructions, the other situated on a table next to the reception desk underneath a night lamp with a sign explaining exactly what to do.

Instead of using either of the telephones to summon help from the sleeping night staff, Mr. Dumpton thought it was sensible to venture out in the pouring rain and brave the wind and try to find his key or some staff. It is unclear exactly what drove him to believe that he would find either of these outside the hotel just before midnight!

Leaving the main hotel door he made his way out over the courtyard area and in doing so somehow contrived to fall in our ornamental carp pond. Having been gone some time, his wife had managed to work out how to dial o on the night phone and the duty staff duly arrived moments later to produce the room key. Marcus went to look for Mr. Dumpton to find him sprawled next to the pond soaked from head to foot in freezing green water and writhing in agony. Marcus, who was our Scandinavian Assistant Restaurant Manager, helped the poor man who was now very much more sober, into the hotel much to the amusement of his wife. The couple said little more before retiring to bed.

The following morning I was alerted to the plight of Mr. Dumpton, who by now apparently needed medical treatment for an injured leg. In his mid-sixties I guessed he had obviously hit the side of the stone pond wall on his way in or slipped on his way out possibly caused by the shock. He was offered transportation to the local Doctors surgery, which he declined in preference to walking there. After his appointment I learned that it had been recommended by our local GP that Mr. Dumpton attended Poole Hospital A&E for an x-ray although it was suspected that he had only a very heavy bruising of the leg. However he never took this advice preferring to enjoy the remaining day and what was left of his visit.

Having filled out the relevant accident forms and reported the injury to the Health & Safety Executive as a 'reportable injury', I took statements from the duty staff. I later carried out another Risk Assessment of the pond area, this is normally done bi-annually, but after such an incident it is important to review any potential risks. The passive Infrared lighting leading from the hotel was fully operational as was the courtyard nightlight that stays on 24 hours a day. Deeming the lighting to be sufficient, no further action was intended.

The couple went on to enjoy our free hospitality by dining in the restaurant and sampling the wine list later that evening. We offered more than the normal pleasantries and the Dumpton's shared a joke or two about the previous night. When they checked-out the following morning I was confident we had done the hotel and the area proud and eagerly awaited the, as I thought, inevitable mention in a National newspaper.

As early spring moved towards the April showers we had received no news of the article. However one day opening the post I was shocked to find a solicitors letter addressed to my Limited Company, the hotel, and myself outlining Mr. Dumpton's intention to sue for negligence. He had apparently sustained a fracture to his leg, which was discovered after his return to London, and he was now in a plaster cast and on crutches. To compound my shock that the husband of a journalist, both of whom were at the hotel on a 'freebee' was going to sue me, I read the long awaited article in a major broadsheet newspaper the same day. Apart from naming the hotel and detailing our telephone number there was no mention (as previously agreed) of anything else. I had seven days to supply the litigation lawyers acting on his behalf the details of my public liability insurance.

Loss adjusters were sent to the hotel and I was asked to give a statement. Marcus had left our employ in this period to travel to Australia to work, so his previously taken written statement was given in his absence. My written Risk Assessment was examined as was the pond and surrounding lighting. Two weeks later I had a lengthy conversation with my insurers who told me that the Loss Adjuster had found the lighting to be 'adequate' but that there was a risk we might lose the case if it went to court. The suggestion was that the insurers settled by way of negotiation before the expense mounted. However much it cost them, court or not, any payout would affect my premiums by claiming on my insurance by some 20 percent per annum thereafter.

The Dumpton's had failed to take either their room key or the Welcome Card with them when they went out. Enjoyed the hospitality in a local public house until asked to leave, made their way back to the hotel and ignored the instructions clearly posted at the front door and repeated at the reception desk. Failing to think clearly after a night at the pub, Mr Dumpton made a stupid decision to find help in a most unlikely and ice-cold place and in doing so injured himself. The couple got a free two-night break in an award winning Elizabethan hotel. Were wined and dined at my pleasure and in return wrote next to nothing by way of the agreed 'advertorial' in the national 'rag'. Taking up one of the many advertisements from the 'Ambulance chasing' law firms they have gained a great deal. All the above and an undisclosable sum, as agreed courtesy of my insurers.

I believed that it was a good opportunity to get some valuable publicity in return but it had cost the hotel dearly. Far from being the author of something nice, Mrs Dumpton wrote next to nothing. Mr. Dumpton though, was, I believe, the author of his own misfortune.

Eventually the Tourist Board paid out for the Dumpton's stay, but only after I took them to the small claims court and winning a judgement for breach of contract by default. They tried to deny any responsibility claiming it was between the hotel and the newspaper, but Basil got stuck in and won because the hierarchy of the country's tourist organisation failed to submit a defence to my claim.

No more awards from them are expected in the near or distant future.

I always rated 'old' car salesman behind Estate Agents and Internet Penis Enlargement Firms as the lowest of the low and who always over promise and under-deliver, but now journalists have their own place in my league of unsavoury professions.

Imagine meeting Basil after he has dealt with any of the above. Whatever you do, don't click your fingers at him.

But even with this catalogue of horrors, there is always one who gets the Prix d'Or............

'It might be helpful to whistle while you work,
less so at your wife, but
definitely not at my waiting staff.'

Andy Hageman

13 (unlucky for some)
Cruella de Vil

"W hat sort of hotel is this?" she exploded. "No air-conditioning, no bathrobes, no concierge and no room service through the night, how did this place ever win anything!"

"Welcome to Mortons House Hotel, Mrs. de Vil."

Every once in a while and more often than I'd like, we take a booking from somebody with higher expectations of us than are realistic. The Guests from Hell. These guests normally stand out well in advance of their arrival because we inevitably receive a huge number of letters, emails and telephone calls, all with more than a scent of sarcasm. Being organised and careful has nothing to do with it. These guests just exude unhappiness, spite, and bile and have no intention of being satisfied with any aspect of the hotel, the food, the service or the miserable weather, however sunny it is outside.

But once in a while we have the one who wins the Golden Award for upsetting, not only Basil, but the entire organisation, not forgetting her partner too.

Cruella had called several times in the months before her arrival, e-mailed twice and faxed us once, Sybil and Sybling taking most of these communiqués. Each ditty of hers contained a long list of requirements, some would've been deemed unreasonable even to a 5 star establishment. Our lowly 3 stars were never going to stand a chance, despite our Gold awards and Hotel of the Year accolades. Sybil tried to point this out to Cruella in our responses to her many demands, but, no doubt out of sheer bloody minded-ness, she came anyway. But we had been warned and I knew I would have to keep Cruella and my wife Sybil apart.

Our guest wanted total subservience and talked down to all-comers including my wife. According to the Basil of Torquay some three decades back, Prunella Scales was able to toast bread just by breathing on it, and, as my Sybil only needs to glare at it to set the fire bells ringing, I thought it wise to keep these two formidable woman from meeting each other.

Walking into our reception was a woman who clearly felt that no amount of plastic surgery was too much, she looked like she'd had so many facelifts she would require a razor to shave the beard that appeared from below. She had a kind of inelegant swagger as she approached me at the desk, before spouting the double-barrelled name I had already expected.

"I assume my room is ready, so take me there and arrange for my luggage to be brought from the car. You do have a porter, don't you?"

I didn't see her click her fingers at me, but I am sure I heard it.

We had prepared for her arrival by asking three housekeepers to 'spring clean' her room and add the feather pillows that were 'a must', replaced the duvet for sheets and blankets and left the mag-azines she had ordered on the bed. We placed an ice bucket in the room for her to chill her own bottle of champagne (one that she re-fused to pay a corkage fee for, she wanted us to open it and supply crystal glasses for her to drink it though) and arranged the bed-room turn-down for later that evening, a service normally reserved for 'spoon salesmen' if we spot them in time. But as I had carelessly forgotten to employ a porter, I'd have to do.

Surely this would be enough for Madame? Wrong again, Basil.

When I returned to the hotel later on the first night of Cruella's stay, I was greeted with details of her initial findings. Written on the pad provided in the room was a double-sided list of complaints. Among these were: the bed is too hard and the pillows too soft. There is not enough natural light. The room is too hot (she wanted a fan to circulate the stale air). There is a fly in the room, which she wanted removed (we never charge extra for these unless they flavour the soup). The steam train was quaint, she acknowledged, but she wanted me to ask the drivers not to blow the train's whistle every time they arrive and leave the station. Poop, Poop!

At the bar she wanted a Vodka that we didn't stock.

"All good hotels stock my favourite tipple, it's no surprise then that you don't," she complained.

She refused the offer of a tray of roasted peas coated with wasabi paste accompanied by fresh olives from around Mediterranean Europe, but took a menu and a wine list to sit and study in the Oak Room.

I followed her with a menu for her poor husband, who by now was looking more like the man Robin Williams described in Good Morning Vietnam, in more dire need of a blowjob than any white man in history. As I left them to choose their dishes for dinner, I heard her complain about the log fire, which was burning brightly in spite of her mood, it being "too hot!" The couple moved away from the favourite seats in front of the Minster fireplace under the carvings.

Returning to the bar, I was met by a couple sipping at their Bombay Sapphire gins.

"You've got your work cut out there," the woman opined and they both laughed. They went on to tell me of the raised voices they had heard all evening from Cruella and her husband next door. I ventured my thoughts that there would be no satisfying the guest in my Oak Room however hard we tried. I also had to say how hard it was for me to understand why these folk come away to spread the misery further.

There is not an hotelier in the land that reacts favourably to unreasonable behaviour, complaint and sarcasm. Most Innkeepers try their hardest until they get bored. Staff often seek an invisible revenge, or the guest might just make a Basil of me and get the verbal middle finger, which is almost preferable to a waiter pissing in your soup. Either way the service doesn't improve with a click of a finger or a whistle at a waiter, trust me.

Having ordered and gone through to the restaurant, things didn't improve.

"I don't like this table and want to sit at another," Cruella said. My French restaurant manager allowed her to inspect the outlook from each of the fourteen tables laid for dinner. Once Cruella had found one 'that would do,' the couple sat and the staff prepared themselves for her next onslaught. She with a face like a smacked arse and he with the fear of God written all over his.

Their fears were not unfounded, serial complainers never stop and Mrs. de Vil was no exception. It's in their genes, I've concluded. Everything that came to the table went back instantly for some reason, as though the waiter had got his braces hooked on the door handle. Too well done, not enough seasoning, lukewarm, you name it, it was wrong. Even the wine from the temperature-regulated cellar was too cold.

Nothing pleased her, nothing consumed by her was good enough and she was intent on making sure everyone, other guests specifically included, heard all about it. The Basil in me was ripe. When I have tried all my charm, and the second biggest personality in the hotel (Barb) fails too, there is little hope but to leave them to Pierre in the dining room. His Gallic *va va vroom* can melt ice, assuming that there is a heart within the woman beating out complaints on her drum. He failed.

The second day of her three-day break was no better. Despite the fact that the hotel was nearly full from a booking taken more than a year ago, Cruella wanted to move rooms, but that option wasn't available. She spent most of the day calling reception asking if there had been a cancellation, given our strict policy on this, an unlikely event. The last time she called she was unlucky. She got me.

As soon as she started the same old record I felt the Basil rise within me.

"Enough Mrs. de Vil, I will book you into another hotel, as we clearly cannot rise to your unrealistic expectations." The spluttering from the other end of the phone was one of shock. She went on to say that she didn't want to move hotels at all, and that she'd cope in our inadequate establishment, despite her issues. But I wanted her to leave, as did all my staff, and I knew just the place.

A few miles from us was a hotel with the same telephone code, the one that couldn't be bothered to forward a cancellation fax that caused me untold bother and a court case during my Annus Horribilus. Now it was payback time. So Mr. and Miserable de Vil were packed off the to The Manor House Hotel in Studland.

Cruella was lucky, I didn't blow my stack, but my revenge was sweet, she had got more than she'd bargained for and would get less than we had offered her, elsewhere.

But I am often left wondering why people behave in a manner that will never, whatever the star rating, get them better service or something for nothing? It is not what you say, how often you say it, but how you say it. I have never seen a waiter piss in the soup but I can imagine it happens when a customer pushes too far or clicks their fingers.

Just once is once too often.

As she left for the taxi she came to me at reception and said "For legal and medical reasons I must inform you that my husband, who is a Doctor, has had an upset stomach. This was probably caused either by dinner or the kipper he ate at breakfast."

I didn't venture any comment, because by now I had had too much of this woman, but thought it more likely to be food he'd had at a wedding reception that they had attended locally, or maybe the good Dr. had also had too much of her vile personality which would surely have been enough to upset the strongest constitution. Unlike him I now couldn't give a shit.

Her parting shot was to insist we shredded her personal details, watching me while I did this. My riposte was to tell her what a waste of time destroying her personal details was, as there were two chances she would ever get a mail shot from me. One was nil and the other not that good.

I suppose Cruella's only redeeming feature was that she didn't get drunk and disorderly, but then again maybe she'd have been a mellow bird when inebriated. But rarely do people's personalities get better when drunk, as I have found out.

14

Drunk and Disorderly

"hy don't you shut up and have another drink, lover!" This is always the best way for a woman to put down her drunken partner who is pretending not to be, drunk, I mean. We may serve 10,000 customers a year who can hold more than water, but very occasionally we serve too much to a few that can't.

A couple fell into the hotel and enquired about room availability for one night. After a late cancellation we only had Room 3, a Character double available; they paid cash and checked-in, they said they needed to sleep off a big lunch. We often take late reservations from the passing trade, normally those who come to the area for the day and want more of what's on offer. The couple did not dine that evening and placed the "Do Not Disturb" sign on their bedroom door. After breakfast they came to reception and asked if they could stay another night. There appeared to be no reason why we couldn't accommodate them, as their room was not booked that evening. The "Do Not Disturb" sign remained on the door all day. The housekeepers were happy to have one less bedroom to service. Basil however started to twitch.

The following morning the couple were checking-out late – as neither had plastic cards to pay their bill, they again preferred to settle for the second night with cash. Thanking us for our hospitality, they left happy. A few minutes later I got a call from Barb, the

Head Housekeeper, who wanted me to come and see the bedroom as the couple had left it. I was greeted at the door by a strong smell of cigarette smoke and alcohol, empty bottles were strewn around the Lit Bateau. Then I saw the remains of a take-away curry that appeared to have been eaten directly off the new bedspread. A picture was missing from the wall, as was the handmade cookie jar and all the bathroom towels. The bedspread had a number of cigarette burns and there was a burn mark in the bedroom carpet. The antique copper waste bin in the bedroom was full of vomit. The bedroom now had an added aroma, more difficult to disguise in a hurry.

I rushed from the bedroom to reception and found their check-in card. I wanted to find a mobile number and check the contact details. Barb meanwhile was trying to keep a brave face when clearing up the mess. This is a hard enough job to do normally, but harder if you are proud of your bedrooms, as she is. The customer had paid cash on arrival and not guaranteed the room on a credit card, something I thought we NEVER accepted. The telephone number given was false, as was the address. The total bill for the room's second refurbishment in three months was £1100 – the bedspread alone was £350, and the carpet £450. I had no opportunity to recover this loss.

The reception staff are not supposed to take any booking without credit card guarantee or a large security deposit if paying with cash. In this case the couple looked perfectly normal and fitted the usual demographic profile even if a little tipsy. These guests just had no idea how to behave, as so many today don't.

My mood was not ready for the next check-in. My fixed grin looked hollow and insincere – I was in a rage but hoped that I could hide it. A familiar couple walked to reception and introduced themselves as Mr. and Mrs. Webb, before saying to me, "We have come for our anniversary as promised, Andy – we got married here last year." I lied when I said that I remembered them well. As I scanned the reservations book they told me they had booked a Character double room because it was a special occasion – to my horror, it was Room 3.

The next best 'under the influence' story was when a couple from the East End of London had booked our honeymoon suite, with its four-poster bed and antique furniture.

They were almost as colourful as their language at reception when checking in, and it seemed unlikely that they had stayed in places like this before. Maybe the special rate we negotiated for them after a last-minute cancellation helped bring us within their budget.

On their first night, after enjoying a Jacuzzi in the room with a bottle of fizz, the couple came down to dinner. They enjoyed the canapés in the bar with a pre-dinner drink or two whilst ordering their meals. As they were one of our later tables, we sat them in the smaller dining room. They attacked a bottle of Chablis as soon as they had sat down, finishing it before starting on the Lebanese red, Chateau Mussar, which was to go with the main courses. The couple were making every effort to make the waiting staff uncomfortable, both with their language and by sending back perfectly good food. Audibly critical of the staff and the chefs, the guests then started to make noises about the foreign staff, as if the English would be better. Calling your waiter "A bloody Frog" tends not to endear guests to those serving them. As the noise level from the corner of the room rose, other diners started to look uncomfortable. Poor Marcus, our Swedish assistant restaurant manager, even though not a 'bloody frog,' was too shocked to ask the customer to refrain from using any more four-letter words. Colin, our GM, wasn't, though, and asked them to be respectful to other guests.

"Fuck off!" he was told. He did so rather quickly, having spoken to our Cockney reveller. Ted was just about to go in and remove the man, when a guest from a nearby table got there first. A massive man with hands like coal shovels and with a torso shaped like a piece of Toblerone now towered above the disruptive guests. He politely explained that if his night were ruined any further by the man's behaviour or language, he'd not take it kindly.

It worked, and the couple left half of their desserts in the restaurant and departed, wobbling sufficiently on the way to waste some of the Lebanese nectar by knocking over the bottle when leaving the Castle Room.

From the Elizabethan manor house they went straight to a local pub, apparently to carry on drinking, as by the time our chefs had arrived for 'last orders', the couple were now screaming obscenities at each other and were asked to leave by the landlord.

Once they had struggled back to the hotel they asked to see Colin, the GM. He arrived at reception in time to hear that the couple, now holding each other up were unhappy with their room, the service and the food. They wanted to check out a day early so Colin told them there would be a cancellation fee for the last two remaining nights. The guy went mad, said he wouldn't pay and asked to see me. I was tucked up in bed oblivious to the entire goings-on, as it was Ted's duty night.

Due to the man's near animal nature, Ted instructed Colin to deduct the cancellation fee from his card that night, which prevented the possibility of him cancelling his card before check-out in the morning.

Once the hangover had really kicked in the couple came to check out and were met by Colin, who (having spoken with the chefs) knew the real reason they wanted to leave early after their row in the pub. Colin told the fellow that he'd debited his credit card for the one night and dinner, along with the maximum amount our cancellation policy would allow, totalling about £800. Our crafty Cockney, who'd unknowingly paid up, was stumped and furious. Not only did he have no recourse, but also Colin let slip he knew why they wanted to depart early after the public row in the Greyhound pub. They withdrew all but one of their complaints, and they stayed for another two nights. They only wanted to dine in the main restaurant.

When we did the table plan for the next two evenings, we were clever enough to sit the rugby player with his shovel-sized hands, who had suffered in the Castle Room the previous night, on the nearest table to the 'honeymooners.'

There was near silence from them on both their remaining nights, thanks I am sure, to the close proximity of the guy with the cauliflower ear.

When they finally came to check-out, they claimed they'd been "treated like criminals" and wanted a "substantial discount." He got nothing from me, except for being told that if he had behaved like that on *my* night, he'd have been treated exactly like a criminal – and arrested.

Weddings are always another dead cert for at least 10 percent of the guests to get plastered. Those that don't fall in the pond attempting to jump from one side to the other 3 feet away, often become amorous with the wrong people. Sometimes they strike it lucky and hit it off with a willing partner somewhere secluded.

My favourite wedding to forget involved my former hairdresser. She and her groom had visited the hotel many times to make the arrangements. I attended most of these with Sybling but resisted the temptation to ask for a wet cut and avoid a trip into Bournemouth.

Everything seemed to be going well until some non-wedding guests appeared at the bar. Both the bride and groom thought the 'exclusive use' they had paid for meant residents too. Guests staying in the hotel are warned in advance to keep out of the way during the ceremony and wedding breakfast but we make clear they are not excluded, to the bride as well.

There were a few too many Ken and Barbie types over-indulging and as I knew the couple and many of the guests worked at the salon I frequented, it was tough to keep saying no to demands for more drinks. The group had a party booked locally and we were expecting just two couples to return later. One guest had been wandering around a private courtyard within the grounds and stopped to piss all over the garden, another was having a drunken yell at two resident guests he wanted to make less welcome than even Basil could. The bride was steaming drunk and the time to depart was long gone. I stopped serving drinks and asked any non-resident guests to leave. This included people from the salon hoping to stay until the last minute. There were just too many drunks and my more important resident diners now joined them. Two types of guest no hotelier would want to meet, those out for a quite romantic meal, staring in front of an open fire with canapés and a sherry, the others drinking Grolsch faster than I can pop the stopper.

Plenty of swearing and name-calling from both bride and groom on leaving but when my unhappy crimper returned, I got a slap. Never serve those you know, and never get your hair cut by someone you have served, especially not a slapper.

Once a taxi dropped off a single gent to check in. Mr. Price had booked a room so that he could attend a party locally. We try to keep tabs on this type of guest because they need to be educated in the house rules, as they often return late and oblivious to everything, run amok. He was reminded that he should take his room key with him if he was returning late because reception was only staffed until 11pm. The key code to the front door was repeated several times and written on his welcome card, which also carried other important information about the hotel. He was also asked to return to his room quietly if he was late. The house has no problem with guests going out and getting plastered, as long as it doesn't affect other guests and staff too much.

When Mr. Price left the hotel, he was smartly dressed and responded politely to the receptionist's question as to whether he had his key and key code. He said that he would be back long after reception closed. True to his word, he returned at midnight. But far from being quiet and considerate, he played the silly bugger, as he was now almost comatose with alcoholic excess. No harm in a little high jinks, but soon other guests were dialling reception to complain. Marcus, our Scandinavian number two at the time, fielded the calls in his bedroom. He gave up trying to placate the guests trying to sleep and Mr. Price, who now wanted to order a pizza.

Marcus came from his warm bed to locate the cause of all the complaints, finding him in the Oak Room refuelling and stoking the fire that had been left to burn out.

"Get me a beer and a pizza!" Marcus declined his demands, asking the chap to go to bed quietly. He was surprised when Mr. Price agreed and left without a fuss. Just over an hour later, more angry guests than before disturbed Marcus in his slumber. This time, the sober guests were being woken up and asked if they knew where our drunk could get a late night pizza. Mr. Price insisted Marcus call him a taxi to take him to his favourite pizza restaurant in Poole. Tired and weary, the Swede had no option but to order the cab and get Mr. Price out in the hope he would return sober, or with any luck, not return at all. When the cab arrived, the driver insisted on payment in advance in cash, sensing a difficult fare. As Mr. Price had no cash, the taxi left. Guiding the guest to his room, Marcus heard nothing more until later that morning when he unlocked the hotel at 7am.

Mr. Price was fast asleep behind the reception desk, half naked amongst a pile of cigarette butts, which had all been extinguished on the carpet. On closer inspection, Marcus found that he had also urinated in the reception waste bin, which wasn't watertight. The scene that followed was one that I am glad I missed, because it would have been a true 'Basil' moment. Just as he was being helped to his feet, three corporate guests came down the main staircase to leave for work.

The guys were greeted with the sight of Marcus clutching his drunken guest under the arms, trying to get him up the stairs to his room. Mr. Price's trousers were around his ankles and just as the groups passed at the bottom of the stairs he said to Marcus, "Don't make me go to bed with you." Poor Marcus was too tired to protest his innocence, but had apparently been propositioned by one of the corporate benders the night before. Mr. Price departed with an apology and a smile for Marcus. We were able to placate the guests he had disturbed. The reception carpet was repaired at considerable cost. We later found that he had put out the fire in the Oak Room with the same method he had used to fill the reception waste bin.

We now note on all their guest histories, "classy when drunk, blacklisted, not welcome back." Fortunately, there are others.

15

Mr. Bean and Friends of the House

Please believe me when I say that the guests we would like to return far outnumber those who get a 'black dot' next to their names in guest history on the reception computer. This denotes 'blacklisted' and means that they are not welcome. To get a black mark, the guests have to do something horrid, or rude, or worse, like not paying; these tend not to want to return anyway. Most of these had the unenviable pleasure of being checked out by me in full Basil mode as nobody else likes to confront a whiner.

Some guests return to see us as if they are on some kind of pilgrimage. One such welcome guest is Mr. Roy Gudge.

He always arrives around the beginning of November, when we ensure there is a log fire burning in the original Minster fireplace, under the carvings by Indonesian sailors. Like many others, Mr. Gudge enjoys the Oak Room.

An interesting-looking fellow with a bowl cut hair style, his demeanour is very like that of Mr. Bean and he even drives a Mini – not a pale green 850cc model though, but a beautiful Mini Cooper S, dating back to the mid-sixties, with Recarro seats and body harnesses.

A train enthusiast, he has a great knowledge of our local steam railway, down to the model, type and speed, even knowing if it should whistle when approaching or leaving the station some 50 yards from the hotel. He is of course happy to tell us when "They get it all wrong," as he is when we do.

He isn't at all demanding, but is both complimentary and hugely interesting – unlike Bean, maybe a little strange, just like Bean. He has a view on everything and enjoys the vista the area has to offer.

One year, he left us with a conundrum: "What is the one thing missing from Mortons House Hotel?" He told us that he'd let us know at a later date. We spent hours on it, but Roy refused to give any clues – until one day I received a package in the post. I opened it with some excitement, only to find a box of porridge oats! It appeared Mr Gudge liked porridge in the morning and wanted us to accommodate him. We did, and it still graces our breakfast menu today.

During our exchanges regarding 'the one thing missing;' I remember asking whether it might have been something about the building and its history, or that of the Castle, besieged by Cromwell's Parliamentarian forces.

On his next visit, he brought me another gift, which he presented at reception on check-in. Contained within the colourful wrapping was a cannonball, dating back to the time the Castle was besieged. It was found locally and could easily have been the one that knocked the roof off. I had a plinth made from walnut and a brass plaque naming the donor of this lovely 'thing'. It now sits proudly behind glass in a recess of the bar.

Sometime later the local planners and council refused our plea to re-open a pathway from the rear of the hotel directly to the train station. This would greatly benefit us, as customers could get directly to and from the hotel and station. The link from London Waterloo to Wareham has been made and the line already extends past the hotel to Swanage. If trains ran regularly the hotel could offer to collect guests directly from the steam train with staff dressed in 1930's railway porter's outfits.

The council said there was never a path and we didn't own the land between the hotel and the train station in any case – end of story as far as they were concerned.

Into the fray came our Mr. Gudge, who, after doing some homework, declared that there was indeed a path. The vicar and the squire of our manor house had used it to travel from the station to either the church or the house. All we needed to do was establish that a 'right of way' existed. So our guest provided an old map clearly showing this.

If the railway companies can ever agree to link the whole line with London Waterloo and figure out who pays for the public liability insurance, we will take the opportunity of sticking two fingers up at the council and re-instate our path, as the squire of the manor can.

'Mr. Bean' wasn't a guest from Heaven simply because he gave us a map and a cannonball. He befriended the staff and owners, engaged in conversation that was either historical or relevant and always interesting, and he was invariably constructive when he made critical comments, as he often did. He never upset other guests and was in every way a special friend of the house.

The Oak Room is a popular resting place during cold winter afternoons; the fire warms the room and the ground floor. After dinner guests relax there and unwind before bed. One couple who seemed to frequent the hotel more regularly than seemed possible was Richard and Beverley Evans.

The couple stayed regularly after an anniversary here, and their favourite room was, of course, the honeymoon suite. They quickly endeared themselves to me by feeling so at home when they were here, which is often all you want from guests – to be so relaxed they feel at home. Richard and Bev never took this too far, like some. They often played Scrabble after dinner in front of the fire in slippers and pyjamas.

They were relocating to a local village from the smoke in town and stayed at my hotel while finding the perfect retreat. The recently married young couple have dined in the hotel many times since they finally found their new home in Langton Matravers. I often wondered whether I could persuade Bev to come and work here on reception. Whilst attending a local fete, I asked her if she would be interested; she smiled and pointed to her bump in her tummy. She had more important things to concentrate on. Great guests to have and fun to serve, the type that when you see their name in the restaurant diary you pray it is your night to work.

When Mr. and Mrs. Mudditt came to stay for the second time, we had just put on a new menu; this was the first time they had tested us since we had gained the second AA rosette for fine cuisine. Some guests can be constructive about new menus; others couldn't seem to care less, only a few are negative, unless none of their preferred options are available.

The size of this menu had been greatly reduced to allow us to maintain the heady standards and possibly gain another accolade. We had seven dishes available for each course and an extra vegetarian option. The then head chef, Craig, and his team were working in an all-new kitchen, designed with his input and advice and costing us around £120,000 or roughly equivalent to the amount stored in the counting house Paddy Burt once cruelly described in the Telegraph newspaper.

All the way through their stay, the Mudditts were happy to give comments in the most helpful way, giving us ideas on the portion size, content, balance and the rest, instead of 'fine' or 'lovely' and at best 'very good', which does nothing to satisfy my need for feedback, or the chef's egos.

They were clearly an educated couple that had travelled extensively, and they knew their way around a menu and wine list. The new menu had received some very positive comments from guests, most of them relating to the Oxtail Tortellini, which I knew would be a hit after taste-testing it in my office.

At checking-out time, they told me how wonderful the stay, the hotel and the food had been, and they would be back. I thanked them for their kind comments and prepared to help them with the luggage to the car. This is when Mr. Mudditt beckoned me over and asked for 'a private word.'

He went on to tell me that, in my business, attention to detail was of paramount importance and that any silly mistakes would make me look bad, especially after such a marvellous weekend. What is the point of refurbishing the hotel, he asked, and investing in the kitchen and staff and then making a stupid mistake on the menu? He made me feel like my old deputy headmaster, Cyril Hughes had, twenty plus years earlier, which is smaller than a man of my size should feel, anyway. I asked him to what he referred. He grabbed a menu from the stand and quoted one of the opening statements. "Traditionally cooked cuisine from around the world with innovations to tempt the pallet," he quoted. "Well, Andy, let's just say that you'd not want to tempt any 'pallet' in your restaurant, as the dictionary might give a definition of this as 'a portable platform often made of wood, to store and transport goods by forklift.' Rather than the one you mean – the palate, which you would find in the roof of the mouth, and could easily be tempted by your menu!"

I have never taken criticism well, but I stood stunned and red-faced. Thankfully, Barb arrived just in time with hugs and kisses and lent a hand to the car, with them and the bags.

Spelling has never been a strong point and clearly my MS Word spell checker wasn't going to help me use the *write* version to grace the menu. I changed the spelling and reprinted the menus, which are now checked by many people before going to print.

A couple of weeks later a cardboard box marked 'private' arrived in the post addressed to me. When I opened it, there was a note from Mr Mudditt explaining the reasons for his comments at checkout, and how he felt that anything 'so nearly perfect' as the hotel could in fact, be perfect with extra attention to detail. He

159

thanked me for my efforts and for a tremendous weekend. Also contained in the box was a wrapped book, a folio copy of "The Innkeeper's Diary", published in 1931 and written by John Fothergill, which proved to be an inspiration. It seems that innkeepers and hoteliers have been around a while and their experiences haven't changed too much, even if the people they serve often have.

Whilst spelling is a challenge to me, my memory is surreal; the skill is not extended to names, but holds true for faces.

A year later, I was doing one of my infamous restaurant walkabouts, playing the owner all over everyone, pouring wine, or, as I put it, "Would you like me to take the air out of your glass?" – a great ice-breaker if you feel the couple are about to start an argument – in such cases you stay at the table and tell a funny story, or ask them an open question about the food (one they can't answer with a single word). On one of these occasions, having come on duty too late for the start of service, I went straight into the restaurant to ascertain what was afoot and if all was well. A couple of tables in, I noticed a woman sulking and her partner looking around the room. Normally, we NEVER sit the lady facing the wall and give the gentlemen the view into the restaurant. What always happens once the honeymoon period is over is that the gent gets to see all that is happening in the room, and it is fascinating - ladies playing footsie, couples arguing, waiting staff dithering, the sommelier decanting wine, honeymooners desperate to remove the table between them.

So, he 'people watches' and his lady gets no attention at all. Inevitably, she sulks and a row follows – no dessert no coffee and no tip! I was determined to help, so, moving into the silence with a beaming smile, I initiated conversation with the lady, who perked up and enjoyed some banter. A couple of anecdotes and a joke later, he joined in, and as I left the table all now seemed to be going swimmingly well.

I recognised the people on the next table but couldn't put the name to their faces. I moved towards them and was greeted with two warm smiles. "I see you still have stories to tell, Andy!" – great intro for the next one, which wasn't my best when told to these folks who knew my name. I was about to start on the one about the miserable old bugger who pulled me up for a simple spelling error, but it took me just long enough to draw breath to hear the gentlemen guest say, "How did you enjoy the John Fothergill book I sent you?"

"Hello, Mr. Mudditt! How are you?" That was so close, I remember thinking. Thankfully, they have a sense of humour and enjoy the hotel every time they come, which is often twice a year. They see the Basil in me, but as yet haven't felt his full force. I have only learnt to accept well-meaning critical comments from a few special guests and the Mudditts are special.

As are most of my days, great fun, special, but not always as pleasant.

The Plaza Hotel in New York once enquired Winston Churchill's preferences when he was staying there. The great man replied: "Mr. Churchill is a man of simple tastes – easily satisfied with the best."

16

An April Fool

......................for going to work on Sunday April 1st.

I should never have gone to the hotel. It would have been my late father's birthday and I normally go to his woodland burial site near the little village of Child Okeford to check on his Oak tree.

It happened like this.

0900 – I arrive at the hotel to find all 21 bedrooms at breakfast eating their last Purbeck grills. This meant they would all check-out at once. I had four members of staff working their last shifts before moving onto to pastures greener. 40 people booked for Sunday lunch and another 30 expected for dinner.

0905 – I get a note that the tumble dryer in the staff accommodation is broken. Not important unless the staff need clean dry clothes to come on duty, it seems they do so I take a load over to Syblings and hope she never notices. (Sybling, Ted and the girls are away.)

0910 – Housekeepers report a broken lead pane window in room 8, the bloody neighbours kids throwing apples again I guessed.

0920 – A housekeeper helping out at the busy breakfast is told to F*** off by a demob happy chef de rang. Tears, she goes home. One down in housekeeping.

0930 – The list of 'blown bulbs' is long. I have seven to replace, so I fetch ladders and start, it took me thirty minutes.

1000 – Staff rota not good, we have insufficient staff to clear up and re-lay for an equally busy lunch. So I go to help them.

1030 – I have a wedding appointment interview with a mad couple; I am left hoping they don't book.

1100 – Interview with a local girl who wants to work here, she must be mad too.

1200 – Ready just in time for luncheon. Only a party of nine hadn't turned up. So we rang them to find out why. Answering machine message left.

1205 – The booking that was a 'no show' called the hotel, they had actually booked for the following Sunday, so now we have too many staff this week than we need, made worse that next week is full. Somehow we will have to manage it; it was a receptionist's mistake.

1210 – A party of eleven arrive for their meal in the Castle Room, they had pre-ordered from the menu. The only problem is that fifteen have turned up. In blind panic we relay the private dining room for four more; this is not as simple as it sounds. Basil starts to boil.

1240 – As the restaurant manager places fish cutlery on the table one guest comments that nobody has ordered fish. The pre-order is wrong and has been superceded by another. I print new order from e-mail. This mentions that eleven would pre-order and four would order on the day. So we knew all the time. Chef now boiling. I noted that the receptionist is very quiet.

1250 – An elderly lady from the party in private dining room comes out coughing furiously. Her partner informs me she has Cystic Fibrosis and is regularly sick when she eats! Husband slaps her on the back and she true to form relinquishes her starter all over the bar lounge carpet. The fact that the carpet was cleaned a week earlier did not help Basil's mood. In addition to the Salmon terrine there was also globules of gluey phlegm, as if to garnish.

1300 – Try to move woman from bar to more appropriate place to vomit (like the car park). Staff bring sick bowl from kitchen made by Villeroy Boch. She refuses to move; well actually she can't stand for coughing. Smell and scene not great, 25 other diners file past with mouths agog, but not for long.

1310 – Staff stunned that, having filled the Villeroy Boch bowl in the bar lounge the woman gets up and goes back into the dining room and starts to tuck into her roast beef!

1315 – I have had enough of this, so I ring Sybil and ask her to bring the girls up for lunch in the main dining room as the chef had prepared for nine more than are here. I tell them to be quick as last orders are at 1330.

1350 – My family arrive to my stories and comment that I look a little manic today.

1400 – Order our lunch and continue to tell the girls of my day. I am normally stressed when my daughters eat at the hotel because the staff tittle tattle about the boss too often and I never like giving them innocent ammunition. But I am strangely calm.

1430 – Food arrives, courtesy of a 15-year-old waitress who is sporting a 'Hickie' or love-bite, classy I thought. Nobody on the staff had noticed, so I told the restaurant manager to get her a neck scarf. When he does and tells her why she must cover up her neck, she leaves in floods of tears.

1500 – Party from the other dining room are finished, they leave with my 'sick-bowl' and without a tip, charming.

1510 – My girls order six different flavours of ice-cream and sorbets. I am glad I bought that Pacojet machine for a temporary head chef a few years back, the kids are delighted. Sybil passes on dessert and my daughters say my cheese smells worse than my socks.

1520 – De-mob happy staff about to leave for good are starting to annoy me. Sybil tries to defuse the ticking bomb by changing the tune of our conversation. Basil now entertains other diners with humorous story of his day.

1530 – Sybil gets her way and me home. I run a hot bath and

read the paper, supplements and all until the bathwater is cold.

1630 – Fallen asleep in front of the sport on television, not to be disturbed, and wasn't. I woke to find my girls making me Welsh rarebit for tea. I had hardly enough time to take a quick shower and a change of shirt and tie to get back to the Manor House in time for the evening service. Gentlemen always change their shirt and tie between services, this ensures the customers and the paid help will make note, I change mine too.

But once a fool often a fool.

Especially for going to work for a second time that day.

The restaurant was full, we had even added another table because we had overbooked one couple on a 'discount diner' offer we call the "two for one." Basically you buy one meal and get a second free. It often works beautifully well in keeping the men in white coats busy during the shoulder months of the year when the Grockles become scarcer between Sunday and Thursday.

We were already a bit rushed in the bar as table after table arrived on the scene at a different time to those they had booked. At times like these I earn my crust because how the night goes from a customer logjam in the bar to petit fours later is down to the guy running the front of house operation and his team.

I was just getting a little flustered when one of the restaurant team announced that he had done the drinks, canapés and menus on the two tables by the fire in the Oak Room. A quick check of my crib sheet showed me what I had already feared. I needed to investigate, so off I went wearing a fixed grin rather than the Innkeeper's normal smile.

"Excuse me, while I put another chair-leg on the fire." It's a good ice-breaker (from a Pam Ayres poem) and useful if you haven't greeted restaurant diners at the door of the Manor House. An overly keen 'Manuel' had already seated them in the Oak Room, taken a drinks order, served them with canapés and furnished the group of four with a la Carte menus. Not so useful on this occasion

166

because he had failed to get the name of the booking as the restaurant was already full and the Innkeeper wasn't expecting anymore for dinner.

I didn't recognise the group occupying the seats in front of the fire but they seemed very much 'at home' and were busy perusing the menus.

"What name are you booked under?" I asked with a worried look. "Cartwright, we are booked on your two meals for the price of one offer," came the reply. This was not the reply I wanted as we offer only a limited number of "two for one" specials each night and this evening's allocation had been full for sometime, as was the restaurant. In addition we never offer canapés to 'discount diners' or let them see our a la Carte menu because they think that they can buy one dish and get another free. They have a 'special' menu and no treats.

I checked the restaurant diary and found no trace of the booking; I also looked at the day before and after, even the week ahead and found nothing. I went to ask the restaurant manager if we could squeeze in another table, knowing in advance that the Frenchman would be obliging if he could, before risking the wrath of the overworked man wearing a white coat and a big hat in the snake pit.

With a wag of his crooked index finger and a frown, oh so Gallic I gathered from the restaurant manager shaking his head that there was no space to fit in anybody else when he said "Non." Now "Non" is a very useful French word and the intonation can vary the meaning. This time it indicated that, no, there was no way to fit anyone else in and that yes, I was a twat for asking. He added a few other things as a bonus knowing full well that I didn't understand a word of Frog.

I returned to the Oak Room and told my gin-guzzling clients that we had no booking for them; no room, and they had no chance of dinner here this cold night. I was polite but to the point. These were, *after all* locals, and we do advertise a special dinner offer in the bleak months. This brings in some locals as regular as clockwork, for a few of them it is the only time they come. The idea is that we make little or no money on the food but plenty on the drinks, unless they order tap water (a regular occurrence), which sends me all 'Basil'.

"But I called yesterday and quoted the advert in the local paper as you had advertised," piped up one of the two women in the party. I wasn't taken by her tone, nor the fact that they had polished off the handmade delights they were not entitled to.

"It is clearly your mistake," she said, firmly. As I retreated to the bar to take stock, she added, "They must think we are stupid to turn up without booking" just loud enough for me to hear her.

I expected to return with the same bad tidings. As I was explaining to my receptionist the problem, the two women in the party came marching in and started bawling at me to do something. I first noted that the Basil in me was emerging when they started tucking into the selection of Mediterranean olives on the bar. Instead of using the picks available to select these, they merrily dove in with their fingers. One of the easiest ways to contract some awful tummy bug is to sample the Imperial mints often displayed in a bowl at less salubrious establishments. They are renowned for harbouring all kinds of bugs that can ruin any good memories of your food. The 'ladies' didn't take kindly to my look or the request to cease this Neanderthal technique, and use the picks provided. One had a chip in her nail varnish and the other had one on her shoulder.

Basil was fully in character now, not only had they enjoyed canapés on me, they had no reservation, and were now claiming that I was stupid to have a booking system that had failed so badly. They returned to their seats in front of the fire with sneering looks and left me to sweat on a solution, and to throw out the now soiled olives.

The red mist had descended. Thankfully my reception colleague suggested I call The Manor House Hotel nearby. They are local to us and often copy our 'two for one' dinner offer in the local rag. It is sometimes the case that guests can make an innocent mistake and dial their number instead of ours when booking as we share the same telephone code and have similar monikers. My luck was in; when I called them they had indeed a reservation for four in the name of Cartwright.

Having arrived by taxi and consumed a decent gin and tonic with 'their' canapés, settled in front of the fire and chosen from the a la Carte menu, a four mile trip to a hotel in Studland was not what they had bargained for. As it was impossible for me to fit them in I had no choice but to advise the women of their error and plight.

When I told them that it was indeed their mistake, there were gasps of dismay and a chorus of disapproval, except that my tone was less apologetic now that I knew the facts. "Please don't feel stupid, it is a simple mistake" I said without a hint of glib in my voice.

After paying for the drinks (and canapés) they collected their coats to leave. As one of the now red-faced woman bowled towards the door, wearing a look like a smacked arse, she said "You are both rude and arrogant, we won't be back!" I opened the door to the car park for them now wearing a smug look and they left without further musings. But I was the fool, for going into work on a day made for them.

Whilst I was a little condescending, I was most certainly not rude or arrogant in my dealings with them, but I guess me being right all the time does give rise to this opinion from guests sometimes!

But the customer is always right, just not always in the right hotel.

17

Vintage People and their Vintage Lagondas

fter an inspection by the hierarchy of The Lagonda Club, the hotel was deemed worthy of hosting a 'meet' and we were booked a year in advance. We knew from the inspections that expectations were high and duly touched up the paintwork on the staircase and along one corridor the day before they descended upon us, because it had been commented on last time.

Despite this and the reference to a spiteful hotel review by the turgid Paddy Burt, recently published by the Daily Telegraph, we would be privileged to accommodate the group of 36 and their eighteen vintage Lagondas!

We had previously hosted successfully The Alvis Car Club, and had a Bentley 'meet' and we had the Jaguars to look forward to later in 2007, in both September and November.

Staff and owners cars were ushered away to leave space for the various V12's, 4.0 litres, high chassis' and Rapiers and all other 'comers' in Vintage form. We noted from the early arrivals, that the April 'meet' was normally a wet one, but God is clearly a Lagonda driver, as the clouds parted as if by design and the forecast was for clear blue skies for the foreseeable future.

The Lagonda Club were staying on a special, half-board package, for 4 days, enjoying a different table d'hote menu each day and a breakfast en masse, usually on the dot of 8:00 a.m., before roaring off for an away day on the Isle of Purbeck and beyond. The logistics had been in place for weeks before arrival. The group would order their meals well in advance and sit at 6 tables of 6. The chefs were well versed in catering for the more discerning diner and used the pre-order to their full advantage and prepared meticulously. For the restaurant staff it wasn't so easy, despite the knowledge of who wants what and where they would sit.

I wasn't on duty on the evening of day one, but I understand that it went well, but I wanted excellence. We learned from the lessons of the night before and I was positioned 'on the pass.' This meant calling each meal out to waiting staff as it was finished by the team of chefs, giving specific directions as to the whereabouts of the recipient and his or her name. It went like clockwork but it was more than a bit fraught at times. I consistently had to bellow my instructions to staff in four different languages with more expletives each time, to the fraying at the edges restaurant team. The Lagonda drivers had no idea that there was near pandemonium in the background as their chorus of approval grew by day.

Breakfast duty was a bitch. Nobody pre-orders breakfast and when 36 guests turn up at the same time it usually means hell. True to form even with all the owners on duty it was harder than a busy Sunday morning with more normal punters. Our French staff provided the English owners with a bizarre numbering system for each table so we could deliver the breakfast whilst it was still steaming. By the time I had figured out how the system worked the 'Purbeck grills' were cold, and I was steaming.

Once again, the rather nice car club group had no idea of the panic and as the days passed the system and service got clearer and better.

When everyone had had their fill, they settled into the routine of polishing, loving, and exchanging stories of all things Lagonda, not to mention the tuning, re-tuning, firing up and general preening of the most beautiful machines I'd seen in a while. I was regularly asked for some of "Dorset's finest water" and given a plastic bottle to fill. It took a day or two before I stopped filling these with Hildon mineral water straight out of the bottle, and I wouldn't have stopped had I not seen one being poured into a radiator of a thirsty car.

The head turning appeal of a convoy of vintage Lagondas leaving our car park just after breakfast is hard to describe, but the residents of Corfe Castle, the Stately Homes, gardens, monuments and the A and B roads leading to and from us, were probably as grateful for the sight, as I was. The sight was one to behold, but the noise was a tone that only vintage Lagondas could make, one enthusiast was keen to point out.

During my BMW days my wife and I were crew for the Autohaus balloon that drifted around the skies above Buckinghamshire in the early 90's. Once we were invited to The Balloon and Bentley Festival at Leeds Castle (Kent), I saw some elegant and wonderful machines there, but somehow the Lagondas seemed to radiate more charisma, so much so they kindled my desire to photograph them in all their glory against the backdrop of Mortons House and the clear blue skies. I felt that they 'knew' they were being captured for posterity and seemed to pose for each picture. In total I took around 130 shots and was regularly seen crawling in, under and around the cars to get what I wanted. I almost fell off a 15 foot high wall trying to get all eighteen cars into one picture, vertigo it seems, grows on you with age.

When accompanying one owner, Michael Drakeford on an early morning 'spin' around in his much photographed 'Red Lady', I spotted a good friend and local photographer and historian, Dennis Smale. I knew a wave from such a gorgeous car would be enough of an invitation for him to 'pop in for a coffee.' It worked, and he arrived at Mortons House a few minutes later and helped me with the champagne shot I desired but couldn't take without his help, this being a picture showing the reflection of the hotel in the back of the chrome headlight of the Red Lady.

Having been whisked around the countryside while others enjoyed a Purbeck grill, I returned wanting to drive the scarlet woman, right up until Michael explained that the 'fast pedal' was between the clutch and the brake. A bit too much for an hotelier to cope with, and anyway, I had abandoned the work weary staff on breakfast duty for my own pleasure.

I returned a little later than expected having combed my greying hair and picked the flies from my teeth. I must remember to wear less of a grin next time, however hard that may be. For once the frantic throbbing I felt between my legs wasn't an urge for anything indecent, but the 'good vibrations' from a sexy, six-cylinder Meadows engine beneath me.

It was hard to wave goodbye to the cars after a sun kissed four days, but after that stay, almost as hard to see off their owners, as both had a great time, like me. It was a pleasure 'bump-starting' one out of the car park, quite an event.

An added bonus wasn't the jealousy my daughters showed when I told them of my spin, but that one car club owner and enthusiast stayed an extra night and offered to chauffeur them around in his 1929 2 litre engine 'high chassis' despite the fact that he and his wife had a five hour journey home afterwards. Two more enthusiasts resulted in that little trip; both returned baring a grin full of flies.

Being Basil can be tiresome for many, and me. But after this I felt like it was all worth it. Rarely are customers as beautiful to serve, as their cars are to look at, even when they drive a rusty old Fiesta, but especially when they drive pre-war Lagondas.

The Red Lady is a 1933 M45 the first to be fitted with a Meadows 4.5 litre engine and a T7 tourer body, which was very foxy. Toys for the boys, perhaps, but food for the kids is a much tougher problem.

18

Children for Dinner

"heck on!" I shouted to the chef in his white coat. "And that needs ketchup and mayonnaise as side orders." An order like this is a dead giveaway to the kitchen staff who know that it means we've got rug rats on the premises.

"You got kids for dinner, Basil? How do you want them cooked, fried or boiled?" came the reply. Actually I usually eat children well braised but am given to making pie from them now and again too.

Having children for dinner can be a test of the best wills in the world, but it can be made easier if mine host and the staff try a lot. For example, by engaging the rug rats right away is a starter. I hand them menus, introduce myself and normally ask a silly question, once 'on-board' the rest can be plain sailing. We always sit ankle biters with a view into the restaurant so they can see what's going on. We never give them crayons to graffiti the Egyptian cotton tablecloths. When you take the order it is advisable to ask the parents how they want the meal experience managed. Kid's main course can come with the adult's starters and we often serve their pudding with mum and dad's main course. Oh, the best laid plans of the meek and the feeble.

At times we need to employ the Child Catcher from Chitty Chitty Bang Bang as the behaviour of the modern day sprog from hell is impossible to manage without a net and a lollipop. Often the parents ignore their offspring in the hope that the staff or Basil cope with their antics, despite the chance they may end up in my stew. It is not entirely the fault of the children, mum and dad rarely set the right example.

"Mayonnaise for your boulangère potatoes young lady, and some ketchup for the young man's dauphinoise..." "Oh and lest I forget, the mint sauce for dad's Pomme puree."(in this case a grain mustard mash potato).

The next sight is dad jettisoning his knife and swapping his fork to his right hand. Mashing up the food and shovelling it in just like a Neanderthal. What chance to the youngsters have at such an example, at times like these you wish that the family had dined in the bar earlier. Then one of the children farts loudly and the whole family laugh. The Major sitting at the next table, suited booted and wearing his poppy of remembrance is starting to feel as uncomfortable as Basil now is.

Not making the award winning restaurant welcoming for under five year olds in the evenings helps, but not so at breakfast when all comers of all ages are in need of a sugar fix, and they hunt down the glucose ridden hot chocolate that Basil makes so well. Once brimming with energy they tear around the restaurant oblivious to the 'Elf and Safety' warnings of staff and knock into any stationary object, with mum and dad happily ignoring their antics and sipping at piping hot coffee and eating a Purbeck Grill.

One family at breakfast did themselves proud like this, one morning. The three children with horns were as unruly as imaginable then. First to go was an orange juice dispenser, shedding its contents all over the carpet, a cereal bowl and one guest who was trying to mind his own business. The parents sat and watched, almost laughing at the scene of chaos. Then a wound that Sybil will find hard to recover from...the smashing of her vintage Marmite pot. It was procured by her years back and was the last of its kind. It houses individual Marmite portions and is the envy of many an hotelier if they see it. One of the ASBO's in waiting picked it up and smashed it on the floor. Nobody lifted a finger in Basil's absence, not even the parents, who said nothing. I returned to the breakfast room later to find a pile of china and a piece of chewing gum stuck to the fabric of the chair.

Very occasionally though, and less and less often these days, you meet a guest or family that makes the whole journey really worthwhile. I am still in love with people in general, but I have become more guarded by the minute, the events of the first year here had made this a surety. So it is a pleasant surprise when first impressions are wrong.

A three-day break awaited the Beharrell-Mortimer family, as did our Purbeck suite with Jacuzzi and views over the steam railway station. The booking card confirmed that they would dine each night and 'the eight-year-old daughter wanted to join her parents for dinner in the restaurant.'

As soon as I read this, my heart sank. Not only would she probably try and drown herself while feeding the fish but also I thought we would have difficulties if she made it to the dining table. It would be better to serve the whole family in the bar where ketchup and mayonnaise is a normal accompaniment, I thought.

I have tried hard to get my own daughters to a stage where I could take them anywhere, and I am nearly there, but my girls have just hit their teens, so I am just hoping they remain willing and able to behave when it's expected. Maybe I am praying rather than hoping.

The 'Young Guests Menu' was not an option for this young guest and we battened down the hatches and awaited what we felt would be the inevitable.

I was on duty the first night of their stay and in the bar expecting the worst. When I saw Natasha for the first time, I felt sure that my earlier assumptions were correct. She was petite, slight even, but I noted that she appeared to be very well behaved and beautifully spoken. Ominous, thought I and expected her to sprout horns when she saw the menu, or at least throw a tantrum.

But all seemed well. She accepted the offer of my speciality pre-dinner drink for children without demur and not a mention of Coca Cola. I call this a 'Mocktail.' It's non-alcoholic and contains pineapple and orange juice, lemonade and grenadine, which make it look like the more adult Tequila Sunrise. I delivered the pre-dinner drinks to the family, who were now seated in front of the fire in the Oak Room.

I served the canapés and explained the ingredients to Natasha and left them all an à la Carte menu and our wine list. There is nothing on this menu that the average kid would recognise as being edible, but strangely I felt inclined to translate for her if asked.

When I returned to take the food order, I got a surprise. Far from demanding simple food or requesting chicken nuggets and tomato ketchup, Natasha, without any prompting from her parents, ordered roasted salmon with spiced lentils, served with foie gras and apple chutney. She went on to say that she would like to follow that with the saddle of venison with a smoked bacon and cep casserole, dauphinoise potatoes and a thyme jus, adding that the venison would be perfect if served pink. She even pronounced it all correctly.

I must admit that I was staggered. Few adults are as sure of their menu selection and I just wondered if she was going to manage to do justice to the meal.

I need not have worried.

Clean plates arrived in the kitchen from the young lady, who was now sending notes to the head chef about how wonderful his food was. She hid them in the butter domes and sent them into the 'snake pit' via the waiters. It was nice for the then-head chef, Derek, who seemed amused at the interruptions to the busy service and replied the same way. This young lady could hold court for hours with informed questions to the multicultural staff. Everybody wanted to wait on her table. She wasn't being obnoxious or rude but it was obvious to all that she was enjoying the attention. Her parents looked on (I can only assume) with pride. Their daughter was impeccable in every way.

Ted told me that second night was not much different. She apparently tried the fillet of Scottish beef with a celeriac purée, pickled carrots and a roasted garlic sauce. The waiters again returned to the kitchen with clean plates from the eight-year-old starlet in the restaurant.

When I came to the bar on the family's third night, I had a complaint. Natasha commented that she thought the 'Mocktail' wasn't as good the night before and would like one the same as the first night, "please."

Everyone was shocked when she ordered the squab pigeon as her main course on that evening, not because it's served with boulangère potatoes, braised salsify and a red wine jus, but because the bird is cooked pink and is something of an acquired taste, as bloody birds are, however game.

Again she entertained the waiting staff, and more notes passed between the thirty something head chef and Natasha. No one in the restaurant or kitchen had counted on her plate being clean this time. However this game little bird ate all of her little game bird and still had room for a dessert.

Her mother, Mary, had asked for the recipe and method of one dish, unusually, this was to the delight of the head chef – as such requests are normally dismissed out of hand by chefs in general, but this time, due mainly to me asking on behalf of Natasha, Derek obliged willingly. It is so rare to meet such a delightful girl, her parents must be so proud and delighted at the way she is, but then again, they won't have the experiences I have had in dealing with children Natasha's age, so they might not know how lovely she is to have around.

I got a Christmas card picture with an image of 'Natasha at her harp' taken by her mother which was followed by an invitation with a photograph showing Natasha's reflection over the carp pond, with my girls' favourite fish – Goldie. And she hadn't fallen in! The card invited Derek and me to Mary's exhibition of photography in London.

Thank you for your lovely Christmas card Natasha, and, yes, we do remember you, how could we forget, and hope you come often enough to refresh our memories.

Late in 2007 we hosted the Thurman family again, they brought with them daughter Lisa. She is another rare example of parents getting it right. I have seen her visit three times in less than a year, with mum and dad twice and with her grandparents once. It is not just that the good ones love the card tricks, the attention and the food, well behaved children enjoying themselves are a great advertisement for the hotel that has so much for kids to do locally. When I enquired how things were at 'Lisa's' table, she politely expressed her disappointment that the Pastry chef had taken off his dessert menu the crème brulee she had enjoyed last time. Without a word of warning I asked the man wearing the pudding chefs white coat to make her one for the following night. She loved it and it was worth the effort just to see her smile that wide and get a big thank you. The sort of gal that if she could tip you she would and always welcome back.

Even Basil Fawlty could enjoy guests like Natasha and Lisa. Which makes it a reason to stay in the business. Which is more than can be said for the South West Tourism Board when they handed us a collective raspberry.

19

The Tourism Industry 'Oscars'

And the winner in this category is...Nobody!" Sybil and I had been invited to attend the Southwest Tourism Excellence Awards in, you guessed it, Torquay, Devon. We had been selected as one of two organisations competing for The Accessible Tourism Award for 2007/8.

A total of seventeen categories of 'winners' sat around tables in The Palace Hotel. Each award was either the Gold winner or the Silver runner up. The announcement of every nominee was greeted with a fanfare of noise not dissimilar to those heard when a prize-fighter takes to the ring with spangled boots and tasselled pants.

The journey down to our old stomping ground and The English Riviera took almost three hours, not helped by my SATNAV's refusal to recognise to the term Fawlty Towers, Watery Flowers and even Flowery Twats, although had it found that one I may have needed to go without Sybil in tow.

On arrival at the hotel we were allocated our bedroom to unpack and change for the 'Oscar' ceremony. Participants were invited to wear 'Black Tie' and Cocktail Dresses. Although optional, we knew from Sybling and Ted's appearance when accepting the award for the Small Hotel of the Year 2004/5, that most dressed to kill.

Sybil informed me that as I had failed to pack my dress shirt early enough to try and purchase one in Torquay town centre. Having parked, we traipsed towards Debenhams. On the way we passed a plethora of local personalities and chavs. Sybil held my hand more tightly than usual after a rather unkempt 'lady' staggered nearer to us than strictly necessary holding a can of high-powered cider. Her dreadlocks smelt almost as bad as they looked. After our brief experience getting to the department store and the purchase of a new dress shirt and cufflinks we decided to get straight back to 'the Palace' to get ready, as Sybil had only three hours before the music started.

On our way back we saw a couple of ASBO contenders fighting in the street, Sybil's fingernails were drawing blood from my now numb left hand. Then we came across the cider swilling dread-locked drunk again, she was now leaning against a wall urinating down her legs. A stream of steaming piss stretched over our path. We hurried back to the comfort of the car and then the hotel.

On our second arrival in our room and on a closer inspection, doubts about the creature comforts started. First there was the radiator, which radiated more heat than necessary but which was impossible to turn off. Opening the sash window we discovered the extractor fans immediately outside, these were pumping smells from the kitchen below at full volume. A couple of short and curlies in the bath and one in the bed brought a frown Prunella Scales would have been proud of, Sybil would stay, but sleep fully dressed, she said.

A mobile toilet seat above a not very clean basin greeted my first ablutions on the toilet. Nothing was boding well as I thought long and hard over some 'business'. I ran myself a hot bath, having cleaned off a tidemark. Sybil followed me into the bath, but when she tried to add more water the shower came on and soaked her Barnet of freshly coiffured hair. The two remaining hours would not be enough, I thought then.

I decided to straighten the toilet seat and re-tighten the fixings. Why, you ask? Because later it may deposit me on the floor if I was well lubricated by 'winners' champagne. A call to reception to ask them to arrange for a man more maintenance oriented than me, to turn off the radiator was greeted with, "Sorry Sir, we can't, the system in your room is faulty." So now was Basil, as it was excruciatingly hot already. I knew then that I wouldn't sleep later, however sloshed. The hotel accommodated so many from the Tourism Oscars that the place was full and there was nowhere for the management to move us, but they did offer us a fan blower to circulate the air within our 'sauna'.

Now hot under the collar and dressed to kill, almost like one James Bond, but not the current one, as I had a middle aged spread and well waxed grey hair. Accompanied by Sybil, looking equally preened, we arrived at pre-dinner drinks only a little late. A quick glance at the table plan and we were asked to take our seats in the lovingly decorated winners enclosure and banqueting room. Sybil liked the look of the menu, compiled using ingredients entirely from the Southwest, wine included and so did I. We met and chatted with our sponsors, also to the other contenders for our award, along with 250 others at 28 tables of Bond Boys and their Moneypenny's.

I have to say that the food and service was in a different league to the bedroom where we wouldn't sleep. Local Salmon and Crab Tians were followed by Devonshire Fillet on hot plates with nicely cooked vegetables. We had a very competent Eastern European waitress called Karolina who fed my desire for more of the good stuff and piled my plate, adding to the ever-bulging cummerbund.

Speeches and music were plentiful as we prepared to accept our award. It seemed to us that we might get a Silver this time, our fellow contenders seemed to have the ideal property to accommodate all-comers, the fit, the well and the less so. As our turn approached, the sponsors from our table went stage bound and we were 'shepherded' to the left of it. Sybil adjusted my bow tie as our category was announced amidst the screaming music now blaring out from the speakers next to my ear.

"And the winner in the category for Accessible Tourism 2007/8 is, neither of these places! There is no overall winner, but two Silver awards go to Mortons House Hotel and Blagdon Farm Country Holidays." Even our sponsors seemed miffed as we retreated to our table.

The ladies representing Blagdon Farm were as surprised as we were and said they couldn't understand what had just transpired. To be honest it probably meant more to them than us. For them, the Gold Award would be a key marketing point, them having 8 specifically designed cottages that are accessible to all. For us the accessible trade is only a very small part of our turnover and the 'Gold' would have been 'a nice to have' but not a key advertising necessity.

One of our award judges was sat silently at our table. A minion sitting next to him had noticed the dismay on the faces of the 'losers'. When she explained that neither of our tourist venues had met the criteria the dismay turned more to anger than anything else. Why? We collectively thought, invite us to attend an award ceremony as winners, in a competition that neither of us could win? Was it political correctness or to keep the sponsors happy? The total cost of our jaunt to Torquay would run into £250 and, to be honest neither 'loser' would have made the trip had we been told the score beforehand. The embarrassing silence at the announcement in the room crowded with penguins in suits and 'Pussies Galore' led us to believe that Southwest Tourism had made a PR faux pas! What they were implying was that there was nowhere within the region which stretches from Bournemouth to Gloucester and down to Lands End that was worthy of a Gold Award. Quite the incentive to encourage less able travellers to visit the area, we moaned! Well done the Tourist Board.

For us the massive investment in building state-of-the-art accommodation had missed the mark, but that didn't stop the Tourist Board using us as the yardstick to train Accessibility Inspectors

(Spoon salesmen) a year or so back in what was expected from accessible tourist venues. The other contenders seemed to be more upset at being overlooked for the top gong however.

To cap the evening off without any popping of corks, the Tourist Board had misspelt Mortons House Hotel. Really excellent these awards! We handed the certificate back and headed for our beds.

The bedroom that greeted us was sweltering. Sybil bedded down fully dressed. An over-hot Basil was only two feet from the raging radiator on 'full hot' despite being set to off. On opening the windows and curtains we now had 1000 watt floodlights trained on us. It was like Colditz, hot, cramped, and no escape. The kitchen fans fell quiet at midnight as the floodlights went dim; the radiator cooled an hour later. I went for one last movement before bed, sitting on the toilet seat I quickly learned why it was previously left loose, as sat straight the seat was so close to the towel rail that Basil burnt his leg, and promptly fell off the throne much to the delight and amusement of Sybil.

Sybil slept more soundly and trumpeted out few noises. I lay awake all night with just a pair of knickers on, which was more than I wanted to wear but I had to protect every orifice from exposure to the creature comforts. At 7 a.m. prompt, on came the fans and the radiator, it became hot and smelly in a trice and the room was uninhabitable very quickly. Basil took a cold shower, we both took breakfast and Karolina again excelled serving the great fare. The food here was very good at least, we commented to each other.

When asked at checkout if we had had a nice stay, we responded politely and asked for our bill. We had agreed to say nothing of our traumas, better act like an Englishmen and fellow hotelier than get justifiably ballistic. The hotel GM greeted us on hearing the stiff upper lip service I employed in my answer. He asked us to detail the problems and quickly admitted that the room was due for refurbishment as part of a massive re-investment plan. He charged us nothing for no sleep and handled us very well. No bullshit or attitude, just honesty and fair play.

Other revellers faired better, clearly there were some lovely, newly refurbished rooms elsewhere in the hotel. Every hotel has at least one room that the receptionists hate to check guests into.

This time it was a fellow hotelier that got a bum steer.

Andy and Ally (Basil and Sybil) accept the Accessible Award from Southwest Tourism and the sponsors.

20

'Tis the Season to be Jolly!'

There is only one thing missing in Corfe Castle once the 'Festivities Committee' has hung our illuminated angels on the gable ends of the Manor House. And that is the snow that never falls.

A more idyllic setting could not be found in this green and pleasant land as the village is decorated as brightly as Blackpool but with quintessentially more taste. The only thing I would change is the piped music in the hotel that fills my head with sleigh bells ringing. This is played for the duration of our occupation for expectant folk looking to party harder than we work.

The 1st of December signifies our start to the festive season and soon after it has begun it is easy to wish it over long before the needles on the Christmas tree fall to the floor. This is because the season to be jolly normally means making most of the hotel staff and the owners decidedly misanthropic.

The men in white coats become quickly bored with preparing rolled turkey breasts, stuffing, roast potatoes, chipolatas wrapped in bacon, bread and cranberry sauce to the hundreds of pre-Christmas parties and goad the waiters to breaking point so even the rock hard brussel sprouts become weapons of mass destruction. The pre-ordered dinners are changed at the last minute because someone has failed to show and the moods worsen in the snake pit.

"Service!" is shouted just as the team of waiters has left the swing door doing what it does best. And if the waiters run, the chefs complain the food will not look right when it arrives with the partially sloshed (already) diner.

The housekeepers get 'high' on the pot pourri we leave in the rooms, that kind of heady Christmassy blend that gets to you after a few days, they have to put up with it for weeks.

The reception staff bicker over who will get the bum shifts over the festive period, Sybling can't do them all and so her pleading memos for help often go unanswered until she cracks the whip. Christmas morning and New Year's Eve are the worst for obvious reasons.

Local companies who come to celebrate the annual Christmas party fill the hotel prior to the big day. And this can be both the highlight and a low point of their corporate year. The bosses want to say thank you in style and the staff want nothing more than to take advantage of the bosses and often each other. Staff at the Elizabethan manor house serve, smile obsequiously and observe.

One such party that took place at Mortons House in the early years sticks in the mind partly because of the tips that we were left. Whilst I have no strong feelings about tipping, perhaps because I have seen businesses like mine handle them in so many different ways, there seems no solution that is the right one. As I don't get allocated any tips, I listen to staff and customer views and make the best of the situation.

On this occasion, unusually both the company directors were involved in the booking via their PAs and both wanted to control the event their way. The party differed from many that year, as the food wasn't to be our "Cattle market cuisine," as one PA charmingly described our Christmas function menu. For double the price, the food chosen would be lovely and everyone could pre-order.

Presentations and gifts flowed as fast as the fine wine chosen by one of the directors to accompany the food. Speeches by both top dogs made clear the rivalry between them. Even their wives seemed to be trying to outdo each other for they were dressed pretty well for mutton, but the outfits were definitely more suited to younger lambs and a dash of mint sauce might have helped.

There wasn't much misbehaviour, just high-spirited revelry. The 36 invited guests were starting to relax and party poppers were popping, crackers bursting with plastic combs wrapped in entertainingly translated Chinese jokes were scattered all over the table. Empty bottles of both red and white wine were cleared to make space for more. There were no complaints, just wildly abundant compliments from all. The two directors kept asking me for a 'quick word' at opposite ends of the table, to tell me that it was the best 'do' they had had and they wanted to see me right at the end! I remember offering my best jokes to the willing audience, keeping back only the ones that would offend, and ensuring I laughed at the director's jokes louder than they laughed at mine.

The menu they chose came to £40 per head. In addition there were 26 bottles of finer wine than usual, but then this was no 'turkey dinner'. Pre- and post-dinner drinks with sundries brought the total bill to just over £3,500. Both directors agreed in advance of the function to add 15% to the total, for which the staff would be grateful.

After the function and before the staff departed on the minibuses, there were separate groups formed around each director, one in the bar, and the other in the Oak Room. As I went in to say goodnight to the one propping up the bar, he made a loud gesture that would have caught my attention at half the volume, and then said: "That, Andy was fabulous – your staff deserve more than just a tip!" He unrolled a thick wad of notes and unfolded plenty, stuffing them into my jacket pocket and kissing me on the cheek, stinking of cigars and cognac. I thanked him, and left for the other director by the fire. A similar thing happened there, excluding the kiss. This time, I protested that the staff had already been well rewarded by the other director; it was more than enough, as I had also applied the agreed service charge to the bill. This only inflamed the situation, as now he wanted to know how much was in my jacket pocket. Helping himself to the contents of my suit revealed that the sum was £400. "Tight-fisted old bugger," he said, promptly unfolding 'a monkey' and stuffing it into my hand!

I spoke with both the PAs and explained what had happened. They both agreed that I had been open and had told the directors the situation and that therefore I should be grateful and just shut up. They also agreed to book again next year before they left.

£1430.40 was the total tip for that night, so it was very rewarding for the staff. For me, my enjoyment was to have had such a great night with two such happy customers. No not the Directors, even though they had been very happy. I mean the 'couple' I almost tripped over when carrying polished champagne glasses back to the restaurant from the kitchen. The company party had been in the main dining room, but the Castle Room opposite was empty, the door was shut but not locked. The 'couple' had slipped out of the dining room to find peace and quiet for a moment. I walked in carrying a tray of glasses and therefore could not see anything below my waist. I nearly dropped the lot when I walked into a young lass performing a sex act on an older chap. I could just see him in his black tie in the semi-darkness. I put the glasses down on the dumb waiter and left with a smirk. Later in the main dining room the conversation somehow turned to piercings. The guy I had met so briefly, if indistinctly, a moment earlier was asking the same young lass I had nearly dropped 40 crystal champagne glasses on, "Why do girls pierce their tongues, what is the appeal?" She stuck out her tongue to reveal a silver stud for all to see. She then said looking directly at me, "Because it is fabulous when giving fellatio, don't you know?" Needless to say the raucous laughter and the stare directed at me sent me home in a blush. "Sybil!"

Mind you there is a lot worse behaviour than an office affair that starts at the Christmas party. It normally involves free alcohol.

Rarely do companies not foot the bill for the whole evening, drinks included. This gives rise to many emotions that remain suppressed during normal working conditions. The less upmarket Christmas parties, the ones on tight budgets are sometimes the easiest to host, then again, it was one such party that ended in a food fight. Very funny if you are clearing up later with a garden rake so the vacuum cleaners don't clog up, ha ha. Not funny at all if you're the one that gets hit on the back of the neck by a warm mince pie as you leave the dining room, like I did.

Our first Christmas was the best but the hardest so far. We had to do so much business to be able to pay the mortgage and the staff, but everything we did seemed to make us and the customers happy, making it worth the effort.

Our first celebrity guest, one who was about to embark on our three day all inclusive break, had asked us if we could get a piano for her musical partner to play in the Oak Room after dinner each night. Sybling and Ted had a piano at home so before we declined the request we thought we'd have a go at getting it to the Elizabethan Manor house the day before everyone arrived on Christmas Eve.

My mother had bought me a 'sack truck' one Christmas past to aid movement of heavy items. Thoughtful my mother, this gift was not like the unwanted woolly jumper mothers often give grown up sons, this was really bloody useful, especially for an innkeeper with a bad back.

Ted and I unstrapped some men in white coats allowing them to do something mad with us. We would lift the piano out of their front door and out on to the main A351 leading to Wareham. Once on the sack truck we would wheel it up to the hotel door. It took five guys from the snake pit and both Directors to get it there. But the abiding memory was the moment some old biddy came over the brow of the hill in her purple Metro to be met by a piano coming her way on her side of the road. She swerved quicker than we could

191

which was a relief as we nearly spilled our load all over the main road, a real close shave.

A wasted effort as our celebrity guest never went near the thing for the whole duration of their stay, but this was satisfying in its way because they were enjoying the party atmosphere. Guest who were strangers to each other on Christmas Eve were now on first name terms by Christmas day, joining tables together for dinner and the like.

After dinner on the big day, the non-resident intruders left and the residents either slept off their overindulgence or, like one family, carried on a party in the bar. At 4 p.m., the guests were warned that there would be a reduced level of service whilst the staff, owners and our children had a party in the Castle Room. Having laid up the main dining room for breakfast, we were all set. The residents were due for a buffet at 8:00 p.m., served by the only sober chef and a waiter, who looked rather less so. The rest got sozzled along with us, enjoying our re-heated turkey and goose luncheon, crackers and free wine from our suppliers.

Just before the evening buffet, our children had been coerced to perform in front of the guests a rendition from 'The Sound of Music.' This is choreographed by Sybil and her Sybling and has become an annual treat for the guests, but less so for the oldest of our nieces. Lauren now helps with the organisation and not the performance: "It is *so* not cool," she told me.

I had attended many of the rehearsals, so I knew the girls were going to perform the 'So long, farewell' song from 'The Sound of Music.' We had just enough girls to perform a couple of spots each: Lauren, the eldest of my nieces, played Liesl and Friedrich, Livvi played Louisa and Kurt, Jemma, my eldest, was Brigitta and Marta, and Emily, my baby, was Gretl. Ella, the youngest of my nieces and the most beautiful white-haired cutie pie, refused to do anything but look stunning.

The dress rehearsal was at the hotel and was the first time I had seen Ella move during the routine, but she was so shy that we expected nothing of her but to stand still – preferably without her thumb in her mouth throughout. Ted was all prepared to be Georg, champagne in readiness for Liesl's question and "first taste."

When the time came for the performance, the reception area was full. Even Barb and her daughter Sue came to watch. The staff that remained from the party, ringed the residents. The owners sat ready for the cue. The girls didn't look nervous at all in front of the audience that had swollen to more than 40 people. Sybling pushed the 'play' button, and from that point a moving, enchanting performance followed. We had guests, staff and 'Von Trapp parents' in tears. The unexpected bonus was little Ella. She was dressed in a bright red jacket and tartan skirt, with matching blue tights and 'Startrite Mary-Janes', dressed to thrill, only not standing still. She bobbed and weaved to the music, jumping up and down on the spot to the delight of all, singing everyone's parts with the tiny voice that only a 2¾ year old has. When the finale came my daughter Emily was supposed to hold Ella's hand and sing her solo: "The sun has gone to bed, and so must I," leading her young niece up the stairs to feign sleep, before 'Liesl' came and collected them to ascend the staircase. Just as Emily began to sing Ella joined in, her timing exactly as my daughters, right down to the moment they lay 'sleeping'. All the girls then ran through the hotel corridor and came down the fire escape by Room 6 appearing as if by magic at reception again. Just in time to see the tears and rapturous applause, along with rapturous cries of "Encore!" This went as well but was funnier because little Ella was bumped off her feet during the performance leading to more guests, owners and staff in tears.

After the revellers had checked out to detox at home we had the job of returning the piano home. Just as we lost control of the sack truck on the downhill run, we noticed a fast approaching purple Metro. The face of the woman driver was one of complete shock, maybe because the odds of meeting a piano on a main road for the

193

second time in four days was slim, or because we had lost control and she had no idea which way to swerve. Everybody involved closed their eyes and waiting for the crashing sound of Metro meeting Piano with the resultant kindling being scattered across the carriageway. But when the brave opened their eyes there was no carnage, just a clear road home, and a Metro disappearing into the distance.

We were lucky and laughed because, 'Tis the season to be jolly...!"

21

The Rundles

"I won't allow it to happen, I forbid it!" Sat in front of me in the Oak Room was an old man, he was remonstrating with a very crooked, even older looking finger, which he was pointing right at me. The scowl on his face gave rise to my opinion that he was more than determined to test the squire's resolve.

The most local locals to us are, of course, our neighbours. On one side we had the Davis family; whose son has worked for us in the past and now their eldest daughter Rosie works weekends in housekeeping. On the other side Mr. and Mrs. Rundle, who lived in a lovely thatched cottage.

This was my first run-in with Alec Rundle, who I knew was as deaf as a post by my having served him in the restaurant. I had invited Alec round for morning coffee to discuss a proposition. I prepared by lighting the fire and seated him next to it and under the saucier of the carvings. With our homemade cookies and a fresh cafetiere in front of him, all was set I thought. But it soon turned into a quarrel over a commercial-sized firework that a guest wanted to explode at his 40th birthday celebrations in our grounds. Just one firework, albeit the size of a dustbin that would make a bang louder than a cannonball hitting the castle. Alec, who had had a bad experience of noisy fireworks during the previous owner's tenure, objected very strongly.

It was unlikely he would be disturbed by the noise, I thought, but his main fear was the possibility of damage to the thatched roof of his 400-year-old cottage. He won that one at a canter, I had no answers that he understood, accepted or even heard. Our first meeting hadn't gone well at all.

Sometime later, when I was in Clealls (the village store), the shopkeeper, Carol, asked Mr. Rundle how he was getting home – my goodness, she can shout, that woman! She then turned to me and asked me, if I'd escort my neighbour home. Mr. Rundle walked as a man in his 90's would, slowly and with a Zimmer frame. Only by now it was pouring with rain and cats and dogs fell from the sky all over us. Somehow we crossed the road safely despite the traffic. However the 'beeps' from the crossing had ended and the green man had become red long before we reached the safety of the other side, because we moved at a shuffling pace, about the speed of a sick slug.

As we walked the 100 yards towards his home, we passed the hotel. No matter how fast I tried to go, there was no rushing allowed by this old twig, despite the fact that I was now soaked to the skin, knickers, socks, the lot. When he looked up to see my Elizabethan Manor House hotel, the rain was dripping from his nose, he looked extremely pale and cold despite wearing my jacket which I had donated him. He paused for a moment and said, "You know, boy, that place is lovely, so is the food – but the owner is a complete fool, a bloody pyromaniac!"

I didn't have the energy to shout loud enough to tell him it was the same fool who was foolish enough to take an hour out of his busy life to walk him home in the pissing rain, nor did I have the strength to kick him and the Zimmer frame a few yards too far when we finally reached the kerb to get him home.

Alec has had many celebrations here for anniversaries, birthdays and sometimes for no reason at all. I'll never forget the protestations before one such party (his 90th birthday) a short time after 'our' walk together. A whole sirloin of beef had been ordered for his family party, one Sunday lunchtime.

He insisted that the meat wasn't to be cooked beforehand and reheated on the day, something we have never done or thought of doing. On the day itself, he demanded to see the uncooked strip-loin on the morning of his party. It must have taken him an hour to do the 50-yard round trip. By the time he had got home and combed his hair, it would have been time to set off for the hotel and his party.

Alec visited the hotel regularly, always accompanied by his wife 'Bill' whose real name is Audrey, and often with his daughters. These two, most local of locals have become the most regular of regulars. I didn't always enjoy their company before I got to know them as it was sometimes hard work as they were always very demanding, and the entertainment value of his views is lost on most fellow guests. Whether it be for luncheon or dinner, there is never any doubt when he comes to visit us because you can hear him as soon as he enters through the front door. Some staff deal better with him than others. Amy, an Australian waitress, very much enjoyed entertaining our closest neighbour, as she spoke at a volume just right for him.

On one occasion Mr. and Mrs. Rundle had booked a table for dinner. They waited in the Oak Room, sipping champagne and eating canapés. This was unusual, Alec normally ordered a sherry to start things off, although 'Bill' often preferred Champagne, so I learnt to substitute her Tio Pepe for something fizzy without Alec noticing.

Colin had to ask three times before being heard, "Are you celebrating something special, Mr Rundle?" The reply was simple, "No." – followed by, "What fresh fish have you today? None of that farmed salmon I had last time, I hope." Colin tried to explain that we had not had salmon as an à la carte main course for the three years since the hotel changed ownership, and if we did ever have it on our 'Two for One menu', it would not be farmed. But he was having to shout so loud that it proved pointless, and now Mr Rundle wanted him to explain what 'Two for One' meant.

By the time he was in the restaurant, my job at the front of house had finished, and I was ready to start my customer service walkabout in the restaurant. On the first table were the Rundles. He had sent his soup back to the kitchen because it was cold. I checked the soup personally, as Alec had asked me to. It was as cold as it was on the three previous occasions on which he had dined from this menu. He had sent back his Gazpacho again because it was cold! We had even changed the menu to read 'chilled Gazpacho', but it didn't matter to him. "The chef is trying to 'swizz' me by serving cold soup again." I offered, at full volume, some tomato and basil soup instead, Alec and 'Bill' accepted my offer of an alternative. When the steaming bowls arrived, 'Bill' said she didn't like tomato soup. You get the picture!

After replacing their soups a second time with a foie gras terrine, I poured some more champagne into their glasses and asked if they were celebrating anything special. 'Bill' smiled at me and said it was their wedding anniversary. When I pressed the point and asked how many years had they been happily married she replied, "I can't remember." Alec, however, wagered it was the 66th! He asked me to join them for a glass, telling me how wonderful the food was and how much he enjoys it every time he comes. He could have fooled me.

We had a lovely one-way conversation, as he never heard a word I said. I learnt about his favourite hotel, Goodwood Park in Singapore. There they served the best, fresh Aberdeen Angus fillet steak in the world, Alec told me. He had sampled this many, many times on his professional travels – and always with a baked potato. I heard many stories of their life together as he made me feel like he really wanted me to know what made him tick. He was right, I did. By the end of the evening he was even calling me Andy.

During this visit I finally plucked up the courage to ask Audrey how she got to get a nickname like Bill. She laughed louder than Alec. She told me that before the Second World War dating wasn't like it is now, and Alec had to cover for his frequent absences from home by telling everyone he was going to see Bill. So it was a great surprise to everybody when Alec told his family he was getting married to a girl called Bill. The name stuck because I never heard her referred to as Audrey.

The last time I saw Alec was when he arrived by taxi for his meal with 'Bill'. I wasn't really shocked because he looked 'a lot' frail. But I managed to explain loud enough that I would willingly collect and deliver them from their home just 50 yards from the hotel, whenever they wanted to dine – I also offered to take round meals on wheels under the silver domes they loved so. I have never made an offer like it before and am unlikely to do so again, anytime soon. But both Alec and 'Bill' had become more than just regulars to me, I really looked forward to them continuing our acquaintance over a glass or two of bubbly.

Just a few weeks later, I was asking Barb whether she has seen either of them recently, when the telephone rang at reception. It was one of Alec's daughters. She asked for me personally and wasted no time telling me that Alec had passed away.

He had apparently insisted that the wake be at Mortons House.

The family had everything arranged except the venue for the 'party' - the church, the vicar, and the undertakers had all settled for a Thursday in August. My heart sank at the news of his death, but almost broke when she uttered that date, 6th August 2007.

I knew immediately that we had a 60th wedding anniversary lunch that day. There was no way we could have this happy party-event and a funeral wake at the same time. Frantic calls and then meetings with the couple celebrating made way for a late afternoon slot to accommodate the grieving Rundles.

I remember thinking at the time, Alec may have insisted his last hurrah was at my place, but nobody thought to ask me if it were possible.

At the funeral I learnt that Alec had been awarded an OBE for services to industry, mainly in Asia - hence his love of Goodwood

Park and that 'Bill's' gong, an MBE, was for services during the Second World War. There was a great picture storyboard telling of his life with Bill and as I had an opportunity to examine this long before the guests arrived I absorbed plenty of it.

He was definitely a Captain of industry, it was probably where he learnt to wave his finger so menacingly, just like my grandfather, a Navy Captain had done a few decades ago. 'Bill' has now moved to a residential home miles away, but near her family.

I will miss them both and hope there are no fireworks in heaven as there were on Earth. Alec was most vocal after a few glasses of champagne and always spoke his mind. He once asked one of my waiters where he came from. When the reply was Persia, Alec said "Do you know the best the thing English gave to Asia and the Far East?" When my now shivering waiter, looking more like Manuel than Andrew Sachs hesitated on a reply, Alec shouted "The English language!" Enough said!

Very often guests make a first impression that is all but good. When the weary hotelier greets such a client, who, for whatever reason has blotted their copybook, it is very unusual for the hosts opinion to change. The Rundles are the perfect example of the very few that did.

Alec died less than a year away from a seventieth wedding anniversary party that would have been a first for us. We have had a few birthday celebrations that featured a letter from the Queen, but they and I missed out on one helluva party for Alec's 100th, I'd planned a feast of Aberdeen Angus fillet with baked potatoes.

Thanks Alec, you were great. Bill has another few years before she gets her letter, and I will toast her myself when she does, I promise.

22

The Passage of Time

If Mortons House could talk, what a fund of wonderful stories it could tell, and if it did, its secrets would change the lives of many. For several hundred years it has watched us humans come and go, laugh and cry, live and die. And it must have chuckled to itself as it watched me turn into an innkeeper not unlike Fawlty.

My part in its history is a mere sliver of time, but it has been a fabulous time and an experience that I would not have missed for the world even though I often felt I had paid the Earth for it along the journey.

Yes, even you, Cruella, I can think of with affection now. And the chefs that so often plagued my life and brought out the Basil in me, all a part of the tapestry, one that couldn't have been woven without my housekeeper's magic. For that, thank you, Barb.

From less than mysterious spoon salesmen to bureaucratic inspectors to wonderful (and not so wonderful) guests, they were a part of my life and I shall remember you all in future years. Natasha, the perfect young guest and old Rundle, the chalk and the cheese in ages. The bouquets and the brickbats that become an integral part of your everyday life, there can't be another profession like it.

Innkeeping is not for everybody, and I dare not ask Sybil, her Sybling and Ted how they see it now, and I thank God my liver doesn't have an opinion.

But for all of you Basil Fawlty wannabees out there, I can assure you – it's a colourful tapestry and a good life.

We are here to serve - but we are not servants.

Acknowledgments and Thanks

So I have told my story, one I hope you have enjoyed half as much as I have reliving the tales, and recalling them here.

I would never have started down the route of Innkeeper had it not been for the support of my parents, Julia and my late father Max. They taught me so much in the days when short trousers were 'in' for twelve year olds, and since have guided me during my time in the motor trade and watched in blind panic as I changed tack to Innkeeper and father.

My great Aunt Sheila with whom I first discussed penning my ideas with, a big thank you for showing enough interest and enthusiasm to get me started, and to Uncle David who must have tired and toiled over my first drafts and incessant questions, your advice and help was invaluable.

To my business partners Bev and Ted Clayton and their delightful children, thank you for adding colour to many of the stories. You deserve a medal for putting up with my style (or not) of management.

Without the constant encouragement and editing of Owen Platt (Bordeaux Basil) I may have given up before getting the job done. Owen read the second draft and oversaw the mammoth changes that were necessary. You're a good man and deserve to be my friend as much as I deserve an invite to the Loire Valley for a tasting of your cellar.

To Thierry Tomassin of Angelus in London, you have always

been a great source of information, knowledge, advice and fine wine. The training you gave my staff and me over the years was absolutely first class. You are a first class restaurateur despite being an Arsenal fan. Looking forward to your next visit with your lovely family my friend.

For my lovely daughters Jemma and Emily and their mother, my wife Ally (Sybil). It has been a long road, one that has not always been straight and smooth. You have always been there when the bumps derailed me, my engine stalled, or a guest thumped me. Thank you.

And lastly to my liver, I am so sorry to have put so much burden on you, and thank you for your extraordinary efforts in getting me thus far.

Andy Hageman,
Corfe Castle, Dorset.
January 2008.